PRAISE GOD, We Won

A Vision of Victory From Jesus Christ in the Revelation

ROGER E. SHEPHERD

WestBow
PRESS
A DIVISION OF THOMAS NELSON

WestBow Press books may be ordered through booksellers or by contacting:

WestBow Press
A Division of Thomas Nelson
1663 Liberty Drive
Bloomington, IN 47403
www.westbowpress.com
1-(866) 928-1240

ISBN: 978-1-4497-3042-0 (sc)
ISBN: 978-1-4497-3043-7 (hc)
ISBN: 978-1-4497-3041-3 (e)

Library of Congress Control Number: 2011919850

Printed in the United States of America

WestBow Press rev. date: 12/08/2011

Contents

Acknowledgements

I express my gratitude to Dr. William Woodson for serving as chairman of my thesis committee. Dr. Bill Goree and Dr. John Parker served as second and third readers. The comments and corrections made by these men were very helpful in my writing the final form of this manuscript. It is with great appreciation that I receive their scholarly insights. Much of this material was first published as a thesis entitled *Victory in Christ in Revelation* by Lipscomb University in Nashville, Tennessee in December, 1995.

The library staffs at David Lipscomb University, Nashville, Tennessee, and Pikeville College, Pikeville, Kentucky, were of tremendous help in supplying much needed resource information. The proofreading done by Ann Carty and Pauline Looney, Pikeville, Kentucky, was invaluable and therefore greatly appreciated. I give a special thanks to Susan Storks and Diann Lazenby for the number of hours they dedicated to the final proof reading, making necessary suggestions and corrections, of this manuscript. I am grateful to the elders of the Main Street Church of Christ, Pikeville, Kentucky, for allowing me the time to do the research for this work. I thank my wife Sharon for her secretarial work, and our children Jason and Lori for their patience in my taking the time away from family activities to devote to this thesis.

List Of Abbreviations

SELECTED APOCRYPHAL WORKS

1 Macc.	1 Maccabees
2 Macc.	2 Maccabees

TIME DESIGNATIONS

AD	After birth of Christ
BC	Before Christ

BIBLE TRANSLATIONS

NIV	New International Version
NASU	New American Standard Update
NASB	New American Standard Bible
ESV	English Standard Version

Preface

This book has been almost forty years in the making. I have always been an optimistic believer in the victory that is only possible through a personal relationship with Jesus Christ. The enthusiasm for this story was set in motion when I completed the theoretical research to complete a master's thesis at Lipscomb University. The attitude of Believers that I have observed through the years is not equivalent to the victory message in the Bible. They need a winning message in order to have a victorious spirit; therefore, a great way to begin is the Nike story.

THE NIKE STORY

The Nike Shoe is definitely a trademark of the faith, commitment, performance, and teamwork that it takes to be a winner in the field of sports. The Nike Company is a fulfilled dream of Bill Bowerman and Phil Knight, professors at the University of Oregon in Eugene, beginning in 1957. Bowerman, one of the top track coaches in America, and Knight, one of Bowerman's middle distance runners, began a relationship that changed the world of sports by capturing the victory concept from Nike, the Greek goddess of victory. The term *nike* connects us to the story of the Nike Shoe Company, illustrating the power to win in Christ. Through *Praise God, We Won!* I intend to promote a positive change in the world, beginning with the church. This book is a focus on the victory over Satan that Believers have through Jesus Christ from the book of Revelation! The Scripture references in this writing are from the book of Revelation unless otherwise noted. The Scripture quotations in this writing are from the New International Version of the Bible (NIV) unless otherwise stated. The word 'Believer' is used to identify those who have accepted Christ in full obedience to the Gospel of God.

Do you feel like a winner? How would you feel if you knew that you could win over all of the battles in life before they take place? You can by reading the book of Revelation! John wrote: "Blessed is the one who reads the words of this prophecy, and blessed are those who hear it and take to heart what is written in it, because the time is near" (1:3). It is now time to embed this beautiful message of daily victory in your heart. You are a winner! This wonderful book teaches you how to win in your spiritual life before it actually occurs. You can win over Satan and all troubled situations in life. You must tell yourself daily, I am successful! I am a winner! *Praise God, We Won!* is a book for those who desire to be victorious in every walk of life.

The last thing on earth that is needed is another commentary on the book of Revelation. This is not a commentary. It is a study of victory in Christ as it relates to daily Christian living. The Believer who seeks to serve God faithfully must know of his daily victories in Christ. This book will enable one to see this victory as a simple message of the Revelation of Jesus Christ. He reveals victory to you in your daily walk to heaven. You are a winner in Christ!

NIKE: THE GREEK GODDESS OF VICTORY

The Greek noun *nike* means victory. This book will concentrate on the verb form (*nikao*) of this word which means to conquer, prevail, or to overcome in Jesus Christ (6:12; 15:2). You are more than a conqueror through Jesus Christ! He will grant to those who "overcome" the opportunity to "eat of the tree of life in the Paradise of God" (2:7). The setting of this biblical concept of victory in the story of Nike, the Greek goddess of victory, is best told in the following story of the Nike Shoe Company: NIKE, pronounced NIKEY. Nike is the winged goddess of victory according to Greek mythology. She sat at the side of Zeus, the ruler of the Olympic Pantheon, in the Olympus. A mystical presence, symbolizing victorious encounters, NIKE presided over history's earliest battlefields. A Greek would say, "When we go to battle and win, we say it NIKE." "Synonymous with honored conquest, NIKE is the twentieth century footwear that lifts the world's greatest athletes to new levels of mastery and achievement. The NIKE "swoosh" embodies the spirit of the winged goddess who inspired the most courageous and chivalrous warriors at the dawn of civilization" (Knight, Nike, Inc.).

The mission statement of the Nike Company is a very simple one: "To be the number one sports and Fitness Company in the world." They have five objectives to help accomplish their mission. First, provide an environment which develops people to maximize their contribution to NIKE. Second, identify focused consumer segment opportunities. Third, provide quality and innovative services and products internally and externally. Fourth, establish and nurture relevant emotional ties with consumer segments. Fifth, maximize profits (Ibid).

Jesus Christ chose the word *nike* to describe the victory of every faithful child of God beginning in the first century. He gave Believers a mission and opportunity of victory in His Revelation. They are quality people rendering innovative services with victorious rewards! Believers can go to battle with Satan anytime and win! We are more than conquerors! Christ is the Master of all levels of achievement. *Praise God, We Won!* is a proper victory motto for Believers in every age who seek to overcome Satan by faith in obedience to Jesus Christ (5:12-14; 7:9-10). He is the Victor! John wrote: "They will make war against the Lamb, but the Lamb will overcome them because he is Lord of lords and King of kings - and with him will be his called, chosen and faithful followers (17:14). You can follow Jesus to daily victory!

NIKE: FAITH, COMMITMENT, PERFORMANCE, AUTHENTICITY, AND TEAMWORK

The Nike Shoe Company, the world's largest marketer of athletic footwear and apparel, is committed to the greatest performance of their shoes. The result is shoes that will set the standard for athletic footwear in the future worn by the serious winning athlete. These shoes have the authenticity of being the bestselling training shoe in the country. The "Just Do It" campaign experiences unprecedented success in increasing Nike's leadership to become the world's finest sports and athletic company. However, the marketing executives did not just create a product, but a lifestyle, a "Nike attitude" (Perez 1). In Christ you can "Just Do It" in successful Christian living! Christ delivers believers to victory now and forever!

One must have faith and commitment to Jesus Christ to be a real winner or victor in this life and in eternity (12:14). Christ expects believers to perform as a team with God, to defeat all enemies by doing His work, in order to win heaven (2:10; 2 Cor. 6:12). The Nike shoe is sold and worn by winners in approximately one hundred ten countries around the world. Christ is worn by Believers to defeat Satan in this present world and to win heaven. The book of Revelation compels people from every tribe and nation to commit their lives to the Lord Jesus Christ with the results of victory over Satan (1:5, 7).

In the midst of Nike's rise as the goddess of victory, Jesus Christ unveiled the beautiful victory story in the Revelation. In the background of the success story of the Nike Shoe Company, people everywhere in every age are challenged to read the victory Christ has over Satan, sin, and worldliness in every battle of life. Praise God, you can win heaven through Christ!

The authentic self is the "you" that can only be found at your absolute core. It is the part of you that is not necessarily defined by your job, your function, your role, your state, or your country. It is the composite of all your unique gifts, skills, abilities, interests, talents, insights, and wisdom. You must believe and see you winning in

Christ! You can become what you believe. Do you believe that victory is achievable? This book may call you to change your authentic self. The only thing in the world you can change is yourself, and that makes all the difference in the world (Cher). Change your thoughts and you change the world (Harold R. Malindon, writer). Remember, positive moments powerfully affirm our authentic selves, inspiring us with an awareness of our own capabilities in Christ. They lift us up to a place from which we can see all kinds of possibilities for ourselves. Do you see the possibilities of victory in daily struggles through Christ? Do you see yourself winning? You can win!

In time of despair we ask, "What can I do for God and my country to make a difference in the success of life and achieve victory through Jesus Christ?" President John F. Kennedy believed in courage, freedom and faith. In his inaugural address, delivered January 20, 1961, he observed that "today is not a victory of a party, but a celebration of freedom-symbolizing an end as well as a beginning-signifying renewal as well as change. For I have sworn before you and Almighty God the same solemn oath our forebears prescribed nearly a century and three quarters ago-the belief that the rights of man come not from the generosity of the state, but from the hand of God" (Patton 5). Victory in Christ is a weapon which Satan cannot duplicate or defeat. Christ is our sun and shield against the world of evil. Victory is a celebration of freedom in Christ! You will enjoy the freedom in the message of this book.

God allows us to be tempted and tried by Satan (2:10). Adversity is one of the most effective tools that Satan is allowed to use for the advancement of our spiritual lives. Many times we see this as a setback, but they are the very things that launch us into periods of deep and intense spiritual growth. Once we understand this principle, and accept it as a spiritual fact of life in Christ, tribulation becomes easier to bear and more productive to our faith in Christ. Therefore, KEEP your chin up and smile. God loves you. He wants you to win!

What is your **purpose** in life? What is your **aim** in life? What **policy** in life do you live by? Have you ever thought about what separates successful Christians who achieve victory from those who suffer defeat? It is the ability to believe there is no survival without victory through Jesus Christ! Christ enables us to be victorious! He gave us the example of doing and accomplishing the will of God in all of His life (John 4:34; 8:29). We have had many national leaders to demonstrate leadership in victory. In Christ believers live with a purpose. They rally around a common cause. Many times during the war Winston Churchill rallied the British people. It all began with his first speech after becoming prime minister:

> We have before us an ordeal of the most grievous kind. We have before us many, many long months of struggle and of suffering. You ask, what is our policy? I can say: It is to wage war, by sea, land and air, with all our might and with all the strength that God can give us; to wage war against a monstrous tyranny, never surpassed in the dark, lamentable catalogue of human crime. That is our policy. You ask, what is our aim? I can answer in one word: Victory-victory at all costs, victory in spite of all terror, victory, however, long and hard the road may be; for without victory, there is no survival (Humes117).

The policy of Believers is to wage war with Satan using the strength and spirit of God. The purpose of God is to produce a fearless assembly of believers who defeat Satan and evil in this present world. The aim of those who walk with Christ is VICTORY!

Roger E. Shepherd

Introduction

FOCUS ON OUR WORLD

The world is in a rage! The economy is hurting, layoffs are prevalent, and society is anxious. Natural disasters continue to multiply. The home is crumbling. Society is in much danger. School is a playground. War is killing its thousands. Terrorism is terrifying to the young and old. Sin is rampant. Satan is filling religion with dogmatism and pessimism. Sickness, disease, and death are marching forward at a great speed. Depression is stealing the joy of many people. In the midst of all this trouble today, there are numerous natural disasters, with tornadoes claiming houses, possessions and lives. A friend reminded me of this despair by asking the question, "What is the world coming to?" My answer in the following pages is to come to Christ! John admonishes, "Come, Lord Jesus", in the beginning and end of the Revelation. Jesus is first to come into our hearts rendering peace and hope of victory. Youth are correctly rejecting "churchanity" and waiting to see Jesus in church. Truly, Jesus is our shelter in the time of storms!

PERSONAL BACKGROUND STORY

My life is one of victory due to the providence and power of God through Jesus Christ. According to the medical statistics, I should have been dead years ago. I have had five automobile accidents that should have been fatal. However, God had another plan. During my senior year in high school, I was involved in an automobile accident that broke my neck at disk one and two in my cervical spine. Most people die with this injury. Twelve years later, I had an automobile accident which broke my neck in the same place. For sure, this would have killed most people. Four years later another accident herniated disk three and four, which later caused a herniated disk in six and seven. Both were later removed by surgery. I was told that I would not survive this accident. Wrong! God blessed me with a speedy recovery. It all ended with another accident three years later that herniated disk five and six. Since then, I still live with this problem plus a new herniated disk at C-five and six, and T-1caused by accident five. God is amazing. The doctors explained to me that, in the cervical spine level one and two, the least touch of a bone or instrument to the spinal cord would bring death. I know God exists. This is the only way I could have possibly been protected against death. He has spared me these many times so I can successfully minister to the lost and edify the believers. I have read of this victory over all enemies, which death is the last one to be conquered by Christ, in the Revelation many, many times. I want you to have this victory!

I have always lived an optimistic life. I believe this is according to the will of God. Christ taught me that "with God all things arc possible" (Matt. 19:26). I can be a positive person with God as my helper. Jesus teaches me by example that having the attitude of a servant, I can always be happy living the life of a believer. Paul taught me that there is "immeasurable" success given to those who believe in the power of God, that works within the human heart (Eph. 3:20). He also taught me that "I can do everything through him who gives me strength" (Phil. 4:13). I know that I can do all things that are according to the will of God through Jesus Christ! He is my Victor! I have the victory over Satan, sin, and self through His blood! God, through Christ and the Holy Spirit, is real in my life. You can have this victory by reading and practicing the principles in *The Revelation of Jesus Christ*.

God is true and real in my life! He has helped me and my family many times in the mission field at home and in the foreign field. The following poem, expressing the existence and power of God, was written by my wife on a trip to Barbados several years ago, while flying across the ocean and islands as a result of meditating on God and His wonderful, mighty creation:

God Is True
As I look over the ocean blue,
It shows God as being true.
The roaring of the beautiful waves,
Was telling me as to say,
God really created me on the third day.
The earth is round and has much water too,
So let me tell you God is true.
If not for God I would not be in place,
but would be flowing out in space.
So look across an ocean blue,
And try to tell me God is not true.
(Sharon Shepherd)

You are encouraged to read the Book of Revelation carefully and thoughtfully in order to gain principles of victory. To give you victory and peace with God through Christ, you also are encouraged to make application of the principles in this work. With daily thought, prayer, class discussions, and application of the message of the Revelation of Jesus Christ, your study should be very rewarding. The book open before us will turn us into optimists. Remember, the pessimist sees the difficulties in every opportunity; the optimist sees the opportunities in every difficulty. This book teaches us to be an optimist! May you experience victorious living every day! You can win! Praise God for His power and glory in our lives!

VICTORY IN CHRIST

It is exciting to win! Everyone enjoys winning at something in life. I was present on December 21, 2000, when the Colorado Avalanche had a great victory over the Los Angeles Kings. The score was five to two. The most exciting win was the fact that Joe Sakic scored three goals in the same game. The hats were thrown to the ice celebrating an exciting victory by thousands of fans who cheered for their team. This was his tenth hat trick in professional hockey. Joe is second on the all time franchise list in goals. He is the 56th player in the National Hockey League to tally 1,000 points and the 14th player to score 1,000 points with the same franchise.

A team can win with the right leadership and power to play the game. How about the game of life now and in eternity? You can win with the right leader and power. Jesus Christ can empower and lead you to many victories in this life and forever in heaven. Praise God! You can win! Is victory important in a sports career? You should ask Joe Sakic. Is spiritual victory important? Let's ask Jesus Christ!

Victory in Christ is a concern of every faithful Believer. I seek to give the meaning of victory in Christ, from the book of Revelation, in words that can be easily understood by all Believers who seek to overcome Satan and the evil in this present world. The book of Revelation is a prophecy of the victory Christ has over Satan (1:1; 22:18, 19). I will concentrate on the verb overcome (nikao) which means victory and to prevail over all enemies.

Winning is everything! Who wants to be a habitual loser? Do we know what it means to win or lose? It is okay to lose occasionally. It is also okay to win! The real question is, "What does it take to win in spiritual warfare?" Do we want to win at all cost? Yes! The cost of victory must be in line with the victory. What we do to win is qualified by the goals or results we desire in the end. Heaven is the goal (Rev. 22). The cost has already been qualified. God paid it all by giving His Son, Jesus Christ, to die for our victory. Christ is revealed in the book of Revelation as the Lamb of God, sacrificed on the cross in Jerusalem for our victory over sin, the world, and Satan (14:1; John

4

1:29). John wrote: "And they sang a new song: You are worthy to take the scroll, and to open its seals, because you were slain, and with your blood you purchased men for God from every tribe and language and people and nation. You have made them to be a kingdom and priests to serve our God, and they will reign on the earth" (5:9-10). John saw the redeemed standing in heaven, rejoicing over the victory Christ won for them by the shedding of His blood at cavalry. Therefore, it is worth our sacrifice to win with Christ (Matt. 16:24)! We must do what it takes to win according to the directions given in the Revelation of Jesus Christ. It simply takes following Christ.

Christ has already won our victory! There was a story told about this victory by a note of encouragement sent to others entitled One Solitary Life: "Here is a young man who was born in an obscure village, the child of a peasant woman. He grew up in another village. He worked in a carpenter shop until He was thirty, and then for three years He was an itinerant preacher. He never wrote a book. He never held an office. He never went to college. He never put His foot inside a big city. He never traveled 200 miles from the place where He was born. He never did one of the things that usually accompany greatness. He had no credentials but Himself.

"While He was still a young man, the tide of public opinion turned against Him. His friends ran away. He was turned over to His enemies. He went through the mockery of a trial. He was nailed to the cross between two thieves. While He was dying, His executioners gambled for the only piece of property He had on earth, and that was His coat. When He was dead, He was laid in a borrowed grave through the pity of a friend.

"Twenty centuries have come and gone, and today He is the central figure of the human race and the leader of the column of progress. I am far within the mark when I say that all the armies that ever marched, and all the navies that ever sailed, and all the parliaments that ever sat, and all the kings that ever reigned, put together, have not affected the life of man upon earth as has that 'One Solitary Life'" (Francis 123-24).

There are many kings and queens in history known for sending people out to die for them, but there is only one King that died for His people. That is the ultimate sacrifice and service of Jesus Christ! I am writing about victory in Christ on the battlefield in everyday Christian living. Rome presented a battle, beginning with the first century Christians, in which they were sorry they were ever born. Man is not able to create an army that can overcome Christ and His followers. He has already declared victory for the people of God. The saints were seen in heaven with palms of victory in their hands clothed in white robes (7:9-10). They had followed Christ in overcoming the kings of the earth. John wrote: "Then I saw the beast and the kings of the earth and their armies gathered together to make war against the rider on the horse and his army. But the beast was captured, and with him the false prophet who had performed the miraculous signs on his behalf. With these signs he had deluded those who had received the mark of the beast and worshiped his image. The two of them were thrown into the fiery lake of burning sulfur. The rest of them were killed with the sword that came out of the mouth of the rider on the horse, and all the birds gorged themselves on their flesh" (19:19-21). Christians have won in Christ! The victory is theirs to claim in Christ!

We choose our freedom in Christ. We choose our peace in Christ. Heaven is reserved in the end for the redeemed that are called by Christ. Victory is only for winners! It is only for those who make the right choices in Christ: "Called, Chosen, and Faithful" (17:14). This is the characteristics remembered by Christ concerning the believers in John's day. How will you be remembered? "If all I'm remembered for is being a good basketball player, then I've done a bad job with the rest of my life" (Isaiah Thomas, Professional Basketball Player). You can make the choice that can change your future state with God. God gives us victory through Christ. Will you choose Christ?

HOW TO WIN IN CHRIST

What can we do to receive the victory in Christ? First, one must **read** the message of the Revelation of Jesus Christ. John wrote: "Blessed is the one who reads the words of this prophecy…" (1:3). The word "read" in this context denotes to read expecting an understanding. God gave us a book that can be understood and obeyed giving us the total victory! The blessings of victory contained in the Revelation of Christ will never secure the faith of the one who fails to read. If you can read you can gain the victory given by God through Christ! You must read for an understanding of the mystery (Eph. 3:4). Reading for an understanding will clear your mind so you can think clearly on the victory that is in Christ. "Victories are won in the mind before they are won on the ground!" (Louis L'Amour).

Second, one must **keep** the things that are written in this book. John wrote: "and blessed are those who hear, and who keep what is written in it, for the time is near" (1:3, English Standard Version). The word "keep" in verse three means to keep with a commitment from the heart. The book opens and closes with this very important message. John wrote: "And behold, I am coming quickly. Blessed is he who heeds the words of the prophecy of this book" (22:7, NASU). A full effort is required to win. "Satisfaction lies in the effort, not in the attainment, full effort is full victory" (Mahatma Gandhi). We must give "heed" or keep His word faithfully. Victors are doers! We must do what Jesus commands to win!

Victors always do the will of God, knowing where and how to walk with Him! Let me share the story of the Welfare Worker who illustrates this point very well. This worker found a crippled little boy in a poverty-stricken section of the city. She took great interest in the boy and longed to see him walk and be a boy among boys.

She decided to consult a famous Orthopedic Surgeon, who agreed to help the child. Examination was made and an operation performed. Slow and tedious days of recovery proved the operation a success. Gradually the child could walk, then run, and then play. He was a boy among boys.

In telling her story the Welfare Worker pauses to say, "He is now a grown man. And I want you to guess where he is and what he is doing?" There are several guesses: "He is now a Doctor. He is a great Humanitarian, a Minister, or a Welfare Worker."

"No, you are all wrong. He is in San Quinton Prison serving a life sentence for murder." Then she continued, "We spent all of our time teaching him how to walk, but failed to teach him where to walk!" This story gives our greater challenges in this life; that of teaching believers where to walk, and how to build our lives according to the will of God. Are you walking with God, keeping His commandments, ready to receive His blessings?

The Believer must always remember; it is the little task when fulfilled, that will give complete victory. So, always keep your eyes open for the little task because it is the little task that is important to Jesus Christ. The future of the kingdom of God does not depend on the enthusiasm of this or that powerful person; those great ones are necessary too, but it is equally necessary to have a great number of little people who will do a little thing in the service of Christ. The great flowing rivers represent only a small part of all the water that is necessary to nourish and sustain the earth. Beside the flowing river there is the water in the earth—subterranean water—and there are the little streams which continually enter the river and feed it and prevent it from sinking into the earth. Without these other waters—the silent hidden subterranean waters and the trickling streams—the great river could no longer flow. Thus it is the little tasks to be fulfilled by all who desire VICTORY!

Third, one must **commit** to faithfulness in battle. Jesus revealed: "Do not be afraid of what you are about to suffer. I tell you, the devil will put some of you in prison to test you, and you will suffer persecution for ten days. Be faithful, even to the point of death, and I will give you the crown of life" (2:10). One must note that his battle is with the Devil. Satan is responsible for trials in life. It is only for a short period of time (ten days). "A crown of victory is given to those who are faithful. The state of faith allows no mention of impossibility" (Tertullian AD 160-230). "Impossibilities that contribute to a fallen

8

state with God are how we deal with them. Difficulties are the things that show what mean [sic] are" (Epictetus, 55-135 BC Philosopher). The possibility of apostasy is within our desire to become unfaithful to God (Heb. 10:26-31). Faith is the victory (1 John 5:4)! There are no impossibilities with God in Christ (Matt. 19:26). Believers must commit to win. In the message of the Revelation of Christ you will understand the battle and how to be faithful to win.

Fourth, one must know his **enemy** who is Satan (2:10). He is identified as "the great dragon", a mythical monster or "the old serpent", "the Devil", and "Satan" who has come to make war with the saints (12:3f; 13:2, 4, 11; 16:13; 20:2). It is so used these twelve times in the Apocalypse to convey Satan's keen power of sight to deceive (Vine 183). The adversary may be the king of the bottomless pit in angelic form, but Christ is King of kings (9:11; 1 Peter 5:8). He is the author of all idolatry, which Christ has no fellowship (14:9-10; Matt. 12:24; 2 Cor. 6:15). He is the deceiver, the destroyer, the evil one, a liar, murderer, the ruler of demons and this world, but Jesus originated victory over these things with everlasting life (9:11; 12:9; John 8:44; 12;31-32; 17:15). It is his mission to make trouble for the people of God. Too long God has been blamed for the trouble caused by Satan in the world. There has been trouble for the children of God ever since the Devil first entered the Garden of Eden. However, God declared victory over Satan through Christ in the beginning of the appearance of the Serpent (Gen. 3:1-15). The story of Revelation Twenty is the complete victory Christ has over Satan. Revelation is a victory song for believers in every age who seek to overcome Satan by faith and obedience to Jesus Christ (7:9-10). It should be studied carefully.

Fifth, victory requires one to have a sense of **purpose**. John wrote: "For God has put it in their hearts to accomplish his purpose by agreeing to give the beast their power to rule, until God's words are fulfilled (17:17). The word "purpose" is the mind of God. The word literally means a royal purpose or the goals, aims, will, and battle plans of the King of kings! God stated His mind in verse 16, that is, to burn the great city that reigns over the kings of the earth to persecute Christians. Victory over Rome has been declared through Christ (17:14). His purpose in life was to do the will of the Father (John 4:34). The apostle Paul also served God with the purpose of living for Christ (Phil. 1:21). "The person who makes a success in living is the one who sees his goal steadily and aims for it unswervingly" (Cecil B. DeMille). The faithful children of God must fight with the same common purpose, that is, to follow Christ to complete victory! Our purpose, goals, aspirations, and mind must be set on following Christ to heaven. Are you prepared for the journey?

Sixth, the church must be committed to **helping one another**. The saints who were being martyred cried out together for help with the brethren being killed for the testimony of Christ. "They called out in a loud voice, 'How long, Sovereign Lord, holy and true, until you judge the inhabitants of the earth and avenge our blood?'" (6:10). Jesus Christ helps us because we are too weak to move forward in battle. This is a benefit of His death on the cross (Rom. 5:6-10). If He helps us, we should help one another with spiritual nutrition which must go to the front line of the battle. However, I must receive the help supplied. We can tear down strong holds of the enemy for ourselves and others through the strength supplied by Christ (Phil. 4:13). Righteousness and faith in Christ exalts the people of God. The church is the family of God winning in life together!

Seventh, in the final analysis of the battle the saints must maintain great **patience**. John calls for patient endurance on the part of the saints who obey God's commandments and remain faithful to Jesus (14:12). John in his writing of this Book declares how the saints win. Patience! Perseverance! Steadfastness! "Thirteen virtues necessary for true success: temperance, silence, order, resolution to patience, frugality, industry, sincerity, justice, moderation, cleanliness, tranquility, chastity, and humility" (Benjamin Franklin). These must virtues and many more are yours by faith in Christ! John had a steadfast faith in God's eternal plan to redeem the lost in Christ's death on the cross. Christ has been crucified for your sins and supplies strength to be faithful. Now, be patient during battle, continue to keep God's word, and heaven will be rewarded!

PURPOSE AND CONTENT

In the message of the Revelation Christ exhorts the reader to remain faithful, especially in the face of hostility from a non-Christian environment. It is rich in theme to warn Believers not to practice immorality, idolatry, and to avoid paganism. These warnings remind faithful believers to be critical of their culture lest they lose their victory. They must depend on Christ for victory, not culture and environment. He rules the world!

The visions of the Book focus upon the future with a threefold pattern which are pictured in this book: First, the persecution of Christians is at hand (6:9-11). Second, God punishes the wicked nations (6:12-17; 14:14-20). Third, one can see the victory of God, Christ the Lamb of God, and the salvation of His followers (7:9-17; 15:2-4). Christianity is characterized by conflict and struggle. These are overcome by following Christ. It gives a future insight that death is only a phase in this struggle, not the end. Jesus is the example of victory in these conflicts of life. In Christ suffering and death is pictured as powerless. Readers will be given hope of winning within the struggle of evil and challenged to distinguish between God's cause and Satan's cause in their daily lives.

CONSOLATIONS AND ENCOURAGEMENTS

"Yesterday I dared to struggle; today I dare to win" (Bernadette Devlin)! The message of the Revelation of Jesus Christ is one of consolations and encouragements. This was the central message given to each of the seven churches of Asia. There are seven blessings given to the Believer in the message given to these churches which are discussed in a later chapter. The number seven, being symbolic for completion, denotes that the Believer will have complete and perfect blessings of victory. We have the comfort and encouragement of Christ and the Holy Spirit in our walk with God. There is no way we can lose! Christianity is for winners!

The Revelation of Jesus Christ was written to give Believers assurance and encouragement of the final defeat of the forces of evil which opposed them and the consummation of all things at His coming. The exhortation and promise given to all the seven churches is addressed to the individual believer in the words: "To him who overcomes" (2:7, 11, 17, 26: 3:5, 12, 21). That is, each one must hear the message of victory and overcome for himself. The word *nikao* in these passages is a law term meaning that every Believer has the power to prevail in Christ. It speaks to them as if they are in a legal action winning when accused of being superior in a judicial cause (cf. Rom. 3:4). Jesus enables them to prevail and conquer in the battle and contest against Satan (Bauer 541). Christ is the means of victory over all enemies starting with the devil. He enables the victor to subdue opposition to win! Indeed, there is in this writing a message of comfort to believers in a troubled world.

The spirit of overcoming is revealed in the Revelation. God gives victory to the doer of His word (1:3). We are reminded of perseverance in the story of the two frogs that fell into a deep cream bow. One was an optimistic soul, but the other one was a pessimist. "We shall drown," he cried without much of a struggle to be rescued. So with a last despairing cry, he flung up his legs and said, "Good-bye!" The other frog with a merry grin said, "I can't get out, but I won't give in, I'll just swim around until my strength is spent. Then I will die the more content!" Bravely he swam until it would seem that his struggles began to churn the cream! On the top of the butter at last he stopped, and out of the bowl he gladly hopped! What is the point? It is this, if you cannot hop out of trials, keep swimming around and churn your troubles into success. Many times it has been said, "A thing could not be done to find out that someone else has just done it!" Someone well said, "Satisfy your want and wish power by overcoming your can't and won't power with can and will power." Success comes in "cans." I can! You can! We can! It is the hearer and doer of the Word expressed in the Revelation that always pleases God!

Victory is dominant in the Revelation. The Believer who perseveres through life to a final victory in Christ will be given many blessings of comfort. This is a promise to the victorious, those who respond in a positive way to the Spirit's teaching and those who remain faithful to God. The victor must not listen to the Spirit in a passive hearing, but make an active response to what he hears. John, in the verses just mentioned, uses the present participle *nikonti* which means a continual victory is promised to the Believer. "It is not the indifferent church member or the infrequent attendee that the promise is given, but rather to the one (individual) who continually overcomes is ultimately victorious in his Christian life" (Strauss 53). Praise God, we win!

THE FREEDOM OF VICTORY

Several years ago I had the awesome privilege to visit the Statue of Liberty in New York City, which symbolizes freedom and victory for the citizens of the United States. A great celebration took place on July 2-6, 1986, on Liberty Island in New York Harbor in celebration of the restoration and re-opening of the Statue of Liberty. The restoration took almost three years to complete and cost millions of dollars. Freedom is very valuable!

President and Mrs. Ronald Reagan, the Prime Minister and First Lady of France were present at this celebration. On July Fourth, the great fireworks display consumed 60,000 tons of fireworks, with countries from around the world participating from prestigious battle ships.

The Statue of Liberty was a gift from France and stands as a symbol of friendship and of the freedom that citizens enjoy under a free government. This gift was presented on July 4, 1884, shipped to the United States in May, 1885, and dedicated October 28, 1886.

The right arm holds a great torch raised high in the air. The left arm grasps a tablet bearing the date of the Declaration of Independence. A crown with high spikes, like a sun ray, rests on her head. At her feet is a broken shackle symbolizing the overthrow of tyranny. In 1903, Emma Lazarus wrote a poem that was engraved at the base, which in part reads: "Give me your tired, your poor, your huddled masses yearning to breathe free. The wretched refuse of your teeming shore. Send these, the homeless, tempests-tossed to me. I lift my lamp beside the golden door."

It was almost 2,000 years ago that Christ, the Lamb of God, was crucified to assure the Believer ultimate freedom from sin and victory in heaven. "Worthy is the Lamb who was slain to receive power and wealth and wisdom and strength and honor and glory and praise!" (5:12). It was on this day that He wore a crown of thorns; His garments were parted and lots were cast; darkness came over the land; the veil of the temple was rent in twain from top to bottom; the earth did quake; the rocks were rent; He was crucified being nailed to a cross; the graves were opened; and many bodies of the saints which slept arose to die no more!

It was through this gift from God we are given freedom of eternal life beginning in the present time. We are given victory in this life and forever. The inscription on the Statue of Liberty gives one hope and a haven to those entering her shores in search of freedom. Jesus lifts forth His hands and says, "This is Jesus the King of the Jews and the King of kings!" (17:14).

I know that God's gift of freedom and victory is real in Jesus Christ. It is by His grace that I live. I look on the bright side of life. Life is good! There is not a day that I live without pain due to the aforementioned accidents. In all circumstances of life, I have learned the secret. . . live victoriously in Christ! Praise God, we won!

In a greater setting and significance, the book of Revelation states the story of God's children winning over the world and all enemies. People in all circumstances are standing on the shore of wickedness offered by Satan through worldliness and tribulation looking for the day of victory. In the following admonition I intend to open the door of faith in Christ with its significance and the story of many who write about this triumphant glory in the existing literature.

⋘ *Chapter 1* ⋙

Praise God For Victory In The Revelation

How significant is victory in the life of a believer in Christ? Let's study the Revelation and discover God's awesome power to grant a triumphant life. The victory over the world belongs to Jesus Christ. The book of Revelation gives the Christian hope of this victory. The reader of this great book is given assurance of the ultimate victory over all his enemies in Christ who is "ruler of the kings of the earth" (1:5; 17:14). He leads His people to final victory over anything that stands in opposition to Christianity. The Revelation of Jesus Christ is a wonderful book replete with hope, comfort, and victory for the people of God in all ages.

In the Revelation of Jesus Christ the saved and the heavenly host are praising God for victory in Christ. This writing contains the following chapters consecutively concerning victory in the Old and New Testaments, in Christ, in the church, and over all enemies. The saved are represented as "the living creatures" giving God reverence in worship for victory in Christ (4:8-11). One will be able to see, as the message unfolds in this writing, that the saved can praise God throughout all eternity because of the victory in Christ over all the battles of life. There is victory, hope, and comfort in Jesus Christ.

The book of Revelation, the only canonical apocalypse of this period, is unique in the New Testament. The title "Revelation" is translated from the Greek word *apokalupsis* which means to reveal, uncover, or lay bare. "It is the removing of the veil to discover the contents that had been hidden from the view of the enemies of God's people. It is apocalyptic in nature because of its use of angelic messengers, symbolic language, prophetic message, and revelation of hope" (Tenney 210-13). "Apocalyptic literature also describes eschatological events such as the resurrection, the coming of Christ and his kingdom, and judgment" (Brown 312). The message remains the same-victory in Christ!

The general purpose of apocalyptic literature was to encourage and give hope. The book of Revelation is prophetic literature written in apocalyptic style to encourage Christians suffering persecution (1:3; 22:17-19). Apocalyptic literature was an instrument of God used in times of persecution to encourage and comfort suffering Christians through a message containing symbols, dreams, and visions.

One must look beyond the symbols of Revelation to realize the encouragement and hope God has in mind for the Believer. It is easier to see beyond the present circumstances knowing that God will intervene to bring all enemies under control. God accomplished this purpose in Christ to Christians in the first century. We can understand this message of victory if we never fully comprehend the symbols. Believers are more than conquerors. They have at least three options in facing the opposition of Satan and the world. They can (1) struggle futilely with the world on their own; (2) surrender to it and be enslaved; or (3) trust in the endless victory that Christ has won for them. Through Him they can conquer every enemy that would hold them back from a full experience of God's good will!

"All human actions have one or more of these seven causes: chance, nature, compulsions, habit, reason, passion, and desire"

(Aristotle). What do you desire? Faith in Christ is a must to succeed in life now and forever!

SIGNIFICANCE OF VICTORY

There was once a young girl named Susie. She was a very beautiful little girl with the most wonderful doll collection in the world. Her father traveled all over the world on business, and for nearly 12 years he had brought dolls home for Susie to love. In her bedroom she had shelves of dolls from all over the world. She had dolls that could sing, dance, and do just about anything a doll could possibly do.

One day one of her father's business acquaintances came to visit. At dinner he asked Susie about her wonderful doll collection. After dinner Susie took him by the hand and showed him these marvelous dolls from all over the world. He was very impressed. After he took the "grand tour" and was introduced to many of the beautiful dolls, he asked Susie, "With all these precious dolls, you must have one that is your favorite. Which one is it?"

Without a moment's hesitation Susie went over to her old beat-up toy box and started pulling out toys. From the bottom of the box she pulled out one of the most ragged dolls you have ever seen. There were only a few strands of hair left on the head. The clothing had long since disappeared. The doll was filthy from many years of play outside. One of the buttons for the eyes was hanging down with only a string to keep it connected. Stuffing was coming out at the elbows and knees. Susie handed the doll to the gentleman and said, "This doll is my favorite."

The man was very shocked and asked, "Why is this doll your favorite when you have all these beautiful dolls in your room?" She replied, "If I did not love this doll, nobody would!"

That single remark moved the businessman to tears. It was such a simple statement, yet so profound because of the love Susie had for this doll. She loved this doll unconditionally. She loved the doll not for its beauty but simply because it was her very own doll.

God loves us the same way that Susie loved her doll. He loves us unconditionally and wants us to win! God loves us not for what we do, but for who we are. We are His children struggling in a troubled world. We can win through the blood of Christ. John wrote: "To him who loves us and has freed us from our sins by his blood, and made us to be a kingdom and priests to serve his God and Father-to him be glory and power forever and ever! Amen" (1:5-6). We never need to earn God's love. He loves us because we are His special creation in Christ. We are free to blossom in a victorious life because God loves us unconditionally. His love has no strings attached! We can win!

Believers in every age, especially the first century, needed a book to assure them victory over their enemies who are led by Satan in this world. The apostle John wrote a message of victory to the seven churches of Asia through signs and symbols with the guidance of the Holy Spirit from the island of Patmos at the close of the first century (1:1, 4, 9, 14; 21:2; 22:8). The children of God were seen in heaven rejoicing because they were "victorious" over those who tried to destroy their precious faith (15:2). The future of the church is secure and her victories are eternal in Christ. The church is not a sinking Titanic. The wreckage of the giant ship was stated in the words of Captain Edward J. Smith: "I could not conceive of any vital disaster happening to this vessel; modern shipbuilding has gone beyond that." The shipbuilder of the assembly of the saints in the eternal city is God (Heb. 11:10). Her future is secure in Jesus Christ! She will prevail over all enemies, even death (Matt. 16:18). The church will be presented to the Father in the end (1 Cor. 15:24). What a victory! What a future!

The significance of this study is to show that believers can overcome persecution through Jesus Christ. Believers can rejoice because they overcome Satan by "the blood of the Lamb" (12:11). John wrote: "He who overcomes will inherit all this, and I will be his God and he shall be my son" (21:7). Believers will prevail in life by faith in Christ. Where is your faith? How strong is your personal faith in Christ? Do you have a positive attitude toward all things?

You can have hope and comfort in all things through Christ! Do you believe that you have this victory?

We need to count our blessings of victory in Christ. Have you ever attempted to count the stars on a clear night? Or have you tried to count the number of waves that roll in from the sea? On that same sea shore, how long would it take you to count the grains of sand that lie before you? Obviously, an attempt to try any of these tasks would frustrate you to no end. In the same sense, when we attempt to count the total number of God's blessings, we discover there is no end. But what a wonderful frustration! Go ahead and try to count all of His blessings. You will discover what King David did: "Many, O Lord my God, are the wonders which Thou hast done, and Thy thoughts toward us; there is none to compare with Thee; if I would declare and speak of them, they would be too numerous (many) to count" (Ps. 40:5 NASB).

The Believers living in Asia Minor during the time of John's writing of the Revelation needed to be comforted because they were suffering persecution from Roman officials due to their refusal to worship emperors, living and dead, as gods (1:9). It was important for John to address this need because it could prevent apostasy among the weaker and less devoted Christians. Today, man must receive the same message of complete loyalty to God, who will give victory over the enemies of Christianity. Does God lead you to greater victory? Is He your Lord and God?

Victory is commonplace in today's society. One can see the word victory written on billboards, automobiles, and in many advertisements. Society is longing for victory. The greatest victory for any society is in Jesus Christ. One must know Christ, love Christ, believe Christ, and obey Christ to win on earth and in heaven! The victory passage in the Revelation is: "They will make war against the Lamb, but the Lamb will overcome them because he is Lord of lords and King of kings-and with him will be his called, chose and faithful followers" (17:14). Jesus Christ must be our Lord, not some political leader, in order to have the complete victory over all enemies! In the time of the Revelation Christians understood the word "Lord" (*kurios*) to mean three things concerning Christ; namely, 1) He is the Master; 2) He is the Teacher; and 3) He is in complete control of their lives (cf. Rom. 10:9-10). This is the daily confession that we must make to be winners in God's kingdom!

We are chosen for victory in Christ. I once new a young man who was chosen, or adopted, by his parents. He was rejected and despised with fellow students at school. He finally could not undergo any more of their harsh criticism. He said, "Guys, I have thought long and hard about your rejection of my adoption. I am proud of the fact that my parents chose me from the adoption agency. Your parents got stuck with you!" We have been chosen or adopted by Christ for eternal victory (Eph. 1:3-7). Praise God for such redemption!

THE SCOPE OF VICTORY

An athlete will lose without a proper focus. Christians must focus on victory. They expect to win. In sports winning is one hundred percent attitude, training, performance, and focusing on victory. In Christianity winning is one hundred percent focusing on the strength of faithfulness to Jesus Christ. The book of Revelation promises victory to every faithful follower of Christ. The Believer is not alone in this world (Matt. 28:20). He is not without strength, hope, and courage. Christ will carry him through to the finish line with the ultimate victory.

The scope of the victory in the book of Revelation is an overview of the need for loyalty to and faith in the victorious Christ (2:10). The faithful have nothing to fear in Christ. Faith, rather than fear, overcomes the enemies of Christianity (17:14). The verb "overcome" (*nikao*) will be studied in detail as it relates to the victory one has in Christ, in the church, and over all enemies. I will survey victory in all these areas throughout the Bible, but the book of Revelation gives the ultimate or final word. The victory of the book of Revelation appeals to people who have broken lives and tattered nerves, when they feel like there is no hope for living. It gives hope to people who are searching for something to inspire them to keep on living and seeking a better world. It directs them to the inward peace that comes from the victory that is found only in Christ. He is pictured as the Victor coming forth conquering and to conquer (6:2). The victorious saints praise Him at the marriage supper for conquering the world (19:1, 11-16). We are defeated precisely because we would be conquerors without Christ. Yes, it is ironic that saints are more than conquerors through Jesus Christ!

The major problem faced in life by the suffering Believer is presented in chapter six. John wrote: "They called out in a loud voice, 'How long, Sovereign Lord, holy and true, until you judge the inhabitants of the earth and avenge our blood?'" (6:10). They are asking God to vindicate their Christian rights. Therefore, they ask, what victory does a believer have over Satan and the world? This question is often asked today by Believers suffering because of the sin that is in the world. In the following pages Christ reveals the vivid picture of the overthrow of evil and the final victory for Believers who are filled with pain caused by Satan (20:10). In the prophecy of this book, the persecuted believer is given a wealth of comfort, hope for the future, and the fellowship of a victorious church through Jesus Christ.

THE APPROACH TO THE STUDY OF VICTORY

The overall view of the victorious Christ in the daily lives of believers will be presented in an exegesis of the victory passages from the text. The main thrust to the approach of this study is from the Greek verb *nikao*. It will be interpreted in its relationship to Christ, the church, and the enemies of Christ. One must first see the meaning of this book to the Christians living in Asia Minor. Then one will ask what it says to Christians living today.

The word *victory* is the translation of the Greek verb *nikao* which is most commonly defined as 'to gain the victory in reference to the church'. The Believers in the first century overcame him by the blood of the Lamb and by the word of their testimony; they did not love their lives so much as to shrink from death (12:11; 15:2; 21:7).

They loved God even in the face of death because He granted them power to win in life. The word *victory* means 'to prevail, conquer, and overcome in reference to Jesus Christ' (5:5; 6:2; 17:14). In reference to the enemies of Christ and His people, it is translated 'overcome' (11:7; 13:7). Satan only seemed to have the victory temporarily. The crucifixion of Christ disarmed his victory completely (Colossians 2:14-15)! Broader definitions and more detailed passages will be given concerning *nikao* in these areas within the text of this study.

The study of Revelation should be approached in light of its meaning to the first century Christians living in the Roman province of Asia (1:4). While there are alternative views concerning the date of the book (AD 54-70), this writing maintains the AD 96 date (Guthrie 948-62). According to Irenaeus the Apocalypse was written at the end of the reign of Domitian, who insisted that he be addressed as "Lord and God" prior to his death in September, AD 96 (5.30.3). It is apparent from the context of the material that the book was written during a time of persecution when the saints were taught to exalt Jesus Christ as Lord and King rather than the emperors (15:3; 17:14; 19:16). It is "the Lord Jesus who rules the world" (22:20)! The late date would have allowed more time for the loss of love, acceptance of the libertine doctrine, growth of complacency, and decline in morals, which is apparent in the seven letters to the churches of Asia (2:1-3:22). The legend of Nero redivivus (13:3, 12, 14; 17:8), a myth that he was not dead but had fled to the Parthians and would return with their support against the empire, would exclude any date before his death and would point to the time of Domitian. This myth was in wide circulation during the reign of Domitian. However, there is a message of victory and hope for the reader today. The material in this book has a beautiful view of the church, the Christian life, and heaven for the believer. A positive view of life and death will result from this study. Christianity is a positive movement with an optimistic view of life and death.

Scholars have taken four basic approaches to interpreting the Revelation: (1) The Preterist View: the fulfillment of Revelation occurred in the first century and ended there. This view centers on the church's struggle with Judaism and Pagan Rome. (2) The Continuous Historical View: the book is a preview of the history of the church and her enemies to the end of time. (3) The Futurist View: most of the events in the book are projected into the future where they will be fulfilled at the second coming of Christ. The various pre-millennial theories generally follow this school of thought. (4) The Spiritualist View: the imagery of the book has no reference to history; rather it is a series of spiritual lessons or principles about divine government and conflict with evil in general (Morris 17-24).

The book of Revelation is addressed to the persecution of the church in the first century, specifically the seven churches of Asia (1:4). It does project future events at the second coming of Christ (20:11-15). It also contains spiritual principles to help the believer in any age deal with sin and evil (12:7-12). Therefore, I am concerned with the spiritual principle of the victory that Christ gives over the enemies of Christianity in any dispensation of time, especially today (17:14). The setting of the book is in the first century when the church dealt with the Roman Empire; however, the principles set forth have a permanent validity.

A SURVEY OF EXISTING LITERATURE

In a general search for meaning in the book of Revelation, you must be aware of the differences of the various views of men who have studied this book. Many maintain the view that this material has no meaning to our modern day. The other extreme is that the book is the key to understanding the Bible. It is not a closed book as some of these views maintain. Many scholars have studied the book of Revelation in the past with various interpretations, yet all of them relate a message of victory. Believers in every age have searched for victory. The following four areas will give interpretations from scholars in different periods of church history that searched for meaning and victory of life in the Revelation of Jesus Christ.

EARLY CHURCH FATHERS

There were two general groups of Christian writers known as Church Fathers who lived victoriously: (1) The Apostolic Fathers were writers who lived and wrote before AD 120; and, (2) The AnteNicene Fathers who wrote before the Council of Nicea, AD 325. These writings are of great value because they are the oldest sources available that testify to the teachings of Christ. I intend to share the message of the writers who searched for meaning in the book of Revelation in both groups of Christian scholars.

The early church gladly received the book of Revelation. Several of the Church Fathers maintained that the book supported the doctrine of millennialism or chiliasm. Barnabas (AD 130) and Papias (AD 150) were among the first to maintain the doctrine that Christ would visibly reign on earth with the assistance of his faithful followers as they sought the meaning of Revelation 20. There has been an increased interest in this book since the time of Justin Martyr (AD 100-165), who also adopted the view that Christ would return to earth to reign in the millennium and sought support for Christ's literal millennial kingdom in Revelation 20. Further, a man among us named John, one of the apostles of Christ, prophesied in a Revelation made to him that they who have believed our Christ will spend a thousand years in Jerusalem (Martyr 81). These writers saw Christ present with believers in the Revelation.

Irenaeus (AD 130-202), holding a similar view with the Roman Empire representing the antiGod power ruling the world, adopted a literal view of the book with some symbolic interpretation (5.29.2). He was emphatically concerned with its apostolic origin and genuineness. He presented the apostles as believers who were very optimistic about winning over the world power of the Roman world. Faith in Christ is the victory!

Victorinus (AD 290-303), who advocated the chiliast school of thought, wrote the first commentary on the book promoting the recapitulation theory which started with Irenaeus. The recapitulation theory was developed by assigning the second and third series of judgments in Revelation as a continuation of the seals, trumpets, and bowls. However, the victory of God's people was on every hand!

The allegorical method of interpretation of the book of Revelation was more important to Clement (AD 95-140), who regarded it worthy to be in the canon, and Origen (AD 185-254), a pupil of Clement and father of Christian philosophy, rather than the literal view that had been given to it by the Jewish apocalyptic. Origen saw the book conveying only spiritual truths or principles to give life meaning. Dionysius (AD 247-265), bishop of Alexandria and scholar of Origen, accepted the book because it was widely used in the church, but rejected its Johannine authorship.

The Donatist Tyconius (AD 390) set a new stage of apocalyptic interpretation. He followed the footsteps of Origen rather than Victorinius in his mystical exegesis of the text, which excluded any literal or historical interpretation and ignored any application to its first century readers while concentrating on the spiritual meaning. Tyconius was enabled to pass lightly over the references to Rome and the persecuting Emperors, which since the conversion of the Empire had ceased to be of special interest, and to fix the attention of the reader upon the world-long struggle between good and evil (Swete ccx). A more literal interpretation was given to the symbols in the book from the time of Augustine (AD 354-430) to the fifteenth century. Contemporary historical events reflected a view that expressed the antichrist as the worldliness of the present church. Nicholas (1400-1464) viewed the book as portraying the entire history of the church from the foundation to the end of time.

THE REFORMATION THROUGH THE RESTORATION

A good interpretation of the Apocalypse was passed over by many scholars during the Reformation Movement which was the religious movement in the sixteenth century that led to the establishment of the Protestant churches. Such an approach was taken by Huldreich Zwingli (1484-1531) who could make no sense of it, while Martin Luther (1483-1546) regarded it as a dumb prophecy, and John Calvin

(1509-1564) never commented on the book. However, these scholars were in pursuit of victory in the struggles of life. They were in search of the meaning of the Bible to the life of the Believer. They searched diligently for future victory!

Francis Ribeira (1570), a futurist with a background in both the Greek and Latin fathers, gave the book an eschatological interpretation. He saw everything following the fifth seal pointing to the end of time and was followed by his brother, Jesuit Alcasar (1614), who interpreted the book in a Preterist view of the victory the church had over Judaism and Paganism. Ribeira took this view in order to oppose the Reformers' identification of the Pope as the

Antichrist. The Antichrist in biblical times were people who rejected Christ (1 John 4:3; 2 John 7). John clearly states this in Scripture. However, victory belongs to Christ and His followers.

In the seventeenth and eighteenth centuries many scholars were busy with the historical meaning of the Apocalypse. Joseph Mede (1627), William Whiston (1706), and Sir Isaac Newton (1732) in England found immediate fulfillment of the prophecy of John from the days of Domitian to their own day. Hugo Grotius (1644) followed in the steps of Alcasar who approached the book from the standpoint of the writer and his time, abstaining from reading into it the events or ideas of the modern day. Jacques Bossuet (1660) was on the papal side and divided the book into three major periods of history: the age of persecution (ch. 5-19), the victory of the church (20:1-10), and the final victory over evil (20:11-22:13) which is important to this writing. Johann G. Eichhorn (1752-1827) at the end of the century suggested that the book was several acts of drama teaching the progress and victory of the Christian faith.

In the nineteenth century, Karl Auberlen (1824-1864) stands out among scholars suggesting that the Apocalypse reveals a philosophy of history and events only as examples of Christian principles. H.B. Swete gives a good summary of the attitude expressed in Germany of the interpretation and meaning of the book. If the Apocalypse of John is a Jewish work adapted for reading in Christian congregations, or a compilation from non-canonical apocalypses, it is a storehouse of first-century eschatology, or a historical monument which throws light on an obscure age (Swete ccxv). It is not a mystery book for an obscure age. It is a book of victory for every age in the history of man. These scholars searched for power to live for Christ daily.

The foundation of the search for meaning in the Apocalypse in the Restoration Movement was led by J. L. Martin (1810-1873). He basically gave the book the historical setting of the entire Bible, which is a history of all nations and great empires on earth from the beginning of time to the end of the world. He portrayed it as a very beautiful book with relevance to its own time and to the world today. We have, in the Bible, as we said before, a history of the time before Moses wrote, and we have, in the last Book of the New Testament, the history of all the time from the date of John's exile, when he saw the Vision in the Isle of Patmos, down until the Lord shall come to judge the world (Martin 41).

Martin maintained that the book was a history of the world in the past, the present, and future. These periods are seen in his three divisions of the book. Part one covers the past in the phrase, "Write, therefore, what you have seen, what is now and what will take place later" (1:19); part two covers the present tense at that time in the phrase "what is now" (1:19); part three covers the future by Jesus telling John to write "what will take place later" (1:19). Therefore, Martin maintained that the Book of Revelation reveals the things which John saw in all ages of time. The message is relevant then and now. It applies to all walks of life.

TWENTIETH CENTURY SCHOLARS

The scholars of the twentieth century searched for hope, comfort, and victory over the world, especially Rome. Henry Barclay Swete (1906) treated the book of Revelation as directly prophetical of the conditions and circumstances of Christian societies beginning with the victory the Asian Christians had over their fears and perils in a persecuting world. In the following way he agrees with J. L. Martin by teaching the Apocalypse as a prophecy answering the needs of the Asian Christians and the Christians of all time:

> So far as the apocalyptist reveals the future, he reveals it not with the view of exercising the ingenuity of remote generations, but for the practical purpose of inculcating those great lessons of trust in God, loyalty to the Christ King, confidence in the ultimate triumph of righteousness, patience under adversity, and hope in the prospect of death, which were urgently needed by the Asian Churches, and will never be without meaning and importance so long as the world lasts (Swete ccxviii).

God is not neutral; He wants you to win! You and I were designed by the Creator for lives of richness and challenge. We were made for achievement and fulfillment. It remains only for us to make it happen in Christ, to bring all the pieces of the puzzle together wherever we live. That begins when we genuinely believe that God has, after all, intended us to live abundantly. The scholars of centuries past found this lovely truth in the last book of the New Testament. Victory is real!

William Ramsey (1905) approached the Apocalypse from the standpoint of the Asian churches and maintained the view that the seven churches made up the universal Church, who was victorious over her enemies. Affirming that this was the chief factor in determining the character of the book addressed to these churches, Ramsey gave a general theme of victory over Imperial Rome to the entire book. The rest of the Apocalypse is occupied with the triumph over the Imperial Religion (201).

Mathias Rissi (1964) holds the view that the Apocalypse portrays the conquering Christ as he dethrones the kings of the earth who oppose Christianity. Christ dominates the book as Conqueror (6:2). However, Rome is only one enemy conquered by Christ. Satan is also among this defeated group (Revelation 20), as are sin and persecution

(1:5; 12:1f). Christ is seen as the Victor on the white horse. Christ came to redeem the faithful Believers. Education alone cannot redeem a society; otherwise the Greeks, the Romans, and the Germans could have demonstrated such redemption most efficiently. History testifies to the ruin of man and his social institutions without the intervention of the God of creation, with which man has no victory over sin and evil.

God knows our sorrows, troubles, and cares. He cares and sent Christ to rescue us from evil (1 Pet. 5:7). He knows our every secret thought and fear. He knows how hard the road can be throughout each passing day. He knows that every sinful heart can still repent and that every weary soul is longing to be free. When our lives on earth are over, He will then share His mercy. He bids us to lay our burdens down because He knows and cares! We must lay our burdens at the foot of the cross and allow Jesus to carry us across the finish line into heaven!

William Hendriksen (1967) argues that the Revelation of Jesus Christ reveals the message that Believers are more than conquerors because God is in control through Christ. According to his view, there is no book of Scripture which more specifically sets forth Christ before the Believer, as the Conqueror of wickedness, rebellion, and unbelief, than the Revelation that John wrote to the church (Rev. 12-13). The freedom is in Christ. There was a fable once told about a wolf that met a big, well-fed house dog one evening. The wolf saw that the dog wore a heavy collar around his neck, and he asked, "Who is it that feeds you so well, yet burdens you with so heavy a collar?" "It is my master," the dog replied. The wolf said, "I would not change places with you, my friend." He went on to say, "Neither would I wear your collar for any master, no matter how well he fed me. The weight of the collar would spoil the appetite. *Half a meal in freedom is better than a full meal in bondage*." Are you bound to evil or to Christ? Christ gives us victory as well as keeping us fed spiritually. What would you sacrifice for such freedom?

Everett Ferguson (1974) maintained that victory in Christ as depicted in the Apocalypse is the key for every Believer to have a glorious and wonderful future. He argues that apocalyptic literature such as the book of Revelation is predictive and serves the purpose of instruction and encouragement for the Believer and the major theme of the book is the assurance of God's sovereignty over the world, his faithfulness to punish evil, and reward the faithful (8). What a wonderful pursuit of victory. People of every age, especially in the 70's, and in the Stalin era, knew that evil has great momentum, but the power of good is immobile. The majority of evil fighters has no power to fight endlessly, and will finally comply with whatever prevails. Praise God, victory in Christ prevails. The evil masses may be content to comply with whatever happens in which there is no victory, but the believer will not! However, the Christian understands that victory over evil is only in Christ!

Apocalyptic literature, such as the Revelation of Jesus Christ, had a special place within scholarship, as represented by Grant R. Osborne (1991), as he placed great emphasis on the symbolism of this positive book; that is scholars who saw this book as a message of hope for the first century saints that looked with pessimism toward the present age awaiting God's intervention of defeat over their great crisis. The book promises salvation or restoration to society. It centers upon reality of the presence and control of God. Therefore, the prayers of the saints who asked for retribution is answered in God's wrath poured out toward their enemies (Osborne 227).

Gordon D. Fee and Douglas Stuart (1993) propose a fresh look at the Revelation through the theological lens which gives it a powerful message not only for the first century but also the twenty-first believers who look for hope and victory for the followers of God. In John's message they connect the church and the state in a collision course; and initial victory appears to belong to the state, but the church triumphs through Christ:

> Thus he warns the church that suffering and death lie
> ahead; indeed, it will get worse before it gets better (6:9-
> 11). He is greatly concerned that they do not capitulate
> in times of duress (14:11-12; 21:7-8). But this prophetic

word is also one of encouragement; for God is in control of all things. Christ holds the keys to history, and he holds the churches in his hands (1:17-20). Thus the church triumphs even through death (12:11). God will finally pour out his wrath upon those who caused that suffering and death and bring eternal rest to those who remain faithful. In that context, of course, Rome was the enemy that would judged (239).

ESCHATOLOGICAL MEANING

Eschatology comes from two Greek words, *eschatos* meaning 'last things' and *logos* meaning 'word, subject, matter'; hence, the doctrine of last things such as death and the afterlife. These terms are used in Scripture to teach the consummation of all things. Eschatology relates to life after death, which gives faith and hope to the suffering Christian. This is exactly what is taught throughout the New Testament, but especially in the book of Revelation. Jesus Christ promised eternal life to the suffering saints in the "crown of life" symbol (2:10), which gives this book meaning in eschatological terms.

The first and most important step toward victory is the knowledge that we can succeed. One of the main purposes for John's writing in Revelation was to offer future comfort and encouragement to persecuted believers. He accomplished this goal first, by revealing their future state of blessedness is gained by a faithful testimony of Jesus even at the cost of their own lives (12:11). Second, he is assuring the readers of the inevitability and imminence of the divine punishment of their persecutors (6:10). In this message of Christ to John, He condemned all types of cultural accommodations between Christians and their pagan environment. He did this by transposing the message into a new key using archaic symbols of conflict and victory, suffering and vindication. He "signified (communicated) it by His angel to his bond-servant John" (1:1 NASB).

This writing will give a synoptic view of the eschatology in the Revelation in such things as the coming of Christ in his kingdom, the resurrection, the final judgment, and victory over death. It differs from the negative features of last things that are found in noncanonical apocalyptic literature because the book of Revelation is an inspired account of the victory over sin and the faithful being rewarded with eternal life in the resurrection. The Apocalypse is a message of the final triumph of truth and righteousness for the saints who hold the truth and defeat Satan through Christ and His church. The resurrection of Christ verifies the triumph of the saints in heaven.

Eschatology, in terms of apocalyptic literature, is always concerned with the study of last things, with death, the end of this present age, and with life in the age to come. In reality it is defined as the belief that the power of evil produced by Satan, who is now in control of this temporal and hopelessly evil world of human history, had its evil rule ended by the direct intervention of God, who is the power of good and who, thereupon, will create "a new heaven and a new earth, the home of righteousness" (2 Pet. 3:13). John, in his writing, gives the complete victory of this entirely new, perfect, and eternal age under God's immediate control, for the eternal enjoyment of His righteous followers from among the living and the resurrected dead (21:1). Death is not the end. It is the beginning in heaven with Christ and all the redeemed!

The New Testament has a Greek setting especially in the Roman Empire. The Roman citizens believed in life after death with many gods. While looking forward to the shadowy realm of the dead, they worshipped the gods, Nike, Jupiter, Minerva, and Roma, being the chief god of the Empire. The eschatological view of the Revelation of Jesus Christ gave the Greek believer hope or assurance of a future life beyond the grave. It gave the Roman citizens faith in the God of heaven. God wins over all these false gods. Praise God, we can win also!

I intend to bring to light what previous scholars have revealed throughout their writings, that the book of Revelation is apocalyptic literature produced in times of persecution as a means of encouraging those who are suffering from their faith. It is not a book on military defense, but one that depicts imperial Rome, the power persecuting Christians, defeated by Christ. Previous scholars have shared a message of positive teaching to help us overcome all struggles in life. They saw the Revelation of Jesus Christ as a guide to direct the Believer into paths of righteousness, peace, and victory in the fellowship of God through Christ.

The Revelation of Christ expresses the insight that reality in general, and the Christian life particular, are characterized by conflict and struggle. A further insight is that death is only a phase in that struggle, not the end. The new and old stories of conflict are reinforced by the example of Jesus. They are models for understanding and coming to terms with powerlessness, suffering, and death. Readers are given hope within these struggles and challenged to distinguish God's cause from Satan's cause in their everyday life. If Believers are to realize victory's high destiny, they must not allow themselves to become contaminated by the immorality, pessimism, and paganism that surrounds the world. They must remain faithful to righteousness in all of life's relationships.

The significance of victory is seen in Christ's ability to defeat death for the Believer (20:11-15). In biblical terms man faces death as a new act of God, not as the repetition of a universal phenomenon (Gen. 3:15). In an examination of these passages, we should conclude that (1) the enmity between the devil and the seed of woman was a complete and perpetual enmity; (2) the serpent is the devil and the seed of the devil refers to the devil or diabolical power as seen in Revelation; (3) the seed of the woman should be taken in an individual sense and refers to Jesus (Gal. 3:16); and, (4) the woman designates, in the literal sense, the only woman who holds a relationship to Jesus as mother to son is, as told in the Gospels, as the Virgin Mary. Yet the universal occurrence of death did not fail to impress itself on biblical man (Heb. 9:27). We will see Jesus conquering Satan in chapter 20 which is also present with us if we will walk with Him along the path which is His. He tells us not to have fear (2:10), not in the tones of

33

condescension of the sage, but with the solicitude of a fellow traveler. Without Christ we fight only to put order and success in our lives temporarily; with Him we are already conquerors!

God hears us when we cry (6:10), "God, I have doubts and fears!" He answers us with our faith in Christ. In all the aforementioned literature review, faith in Christ for victory now and forever is the central thread. Faith in Christ overcomes our doubts, fears, stress, anxieties, and emotional pain. We can cast everything on Him because he cares for us (1 Peter 5:7). He is the Good Shepherd who protects His sheep. We are the sheep of His pasture. He heals the brokenness in life. Therefore, faith is a total surrender to the Lordship of Jesus. Got Faith?!

In the succeeding pages, some of the most relevant features of the book will be presented. Victory is its richest treasure, as it relates to the theme of the Old and New Testaments, to Christ, the assembly of believers, and the enemies of Christianity. The open-minded investigators of Revelation will receive comfort, hope, and ultimate victory in a relationship with God and over all enemies through the life and death of Jesus Christ.

Chapter 2

Future Hope And Victory In The Old Testament

Christ is the hope of Israel! The Old Testament is a book of eternal assurance for every believer. "The theme of the Bible is Christ is coming; Christ came; and Christ is coming again! We are a supernatural people, born again by a supernatural birth; we wage a supernatural fight and are taught by a supernatural teacher, led by a supernatural captain to assured victory" (J. Hudson Taylor). Believers are like an eagle that sits on a crag and watches the sky, as it is filling with blackness, and the forked lightning playing up and down on the earth. He is sitting perfectly still until he begins to feel the burst of the wind and knows the hurricane has struck him. Then he swings his breast to the storm, and uses the storm to go upward into the sky. Away he goes, borne upward upon the wind. That is the way God wants us to deal with life – to be more than conquerors! The Old Testament is a book of victory and future hope. The prophet Isaiah called his people to hope by renewing their strength and said: "They will soar on wings of eagles; they will run and not grow weary, they will walk and not be faint" (Isa. 40:31). The story of victory in the entire Bible will help us turn the storm cloud into a chariot!

The Bible is a book about hope and victory. Does the Bible teach a future hope for the children of God beginning in the Old Testament? I will answer this significant question in the affirmative. God wants His people to win. He directs them to this future hope and victory in the Bible, especially books like Ezekiel, Daniel and Revelation. The Old Testament shows one the hope and the violation, the victory and defeat, of human rights. The divine law and the prophets were clear, but they were often ignored in the history of Israel. With our Lord's coming, the matter of human rights takes on a deeper personal meaning for His disciples. God's word reminds one constantly of the anguish and rights of the oppressed, particularly Believers. Believers must have faith in God's ability to deliver like David, a man after God's own heart, who wrote: "I know that the LORD secures justice for the poor and upholds the cause of the needy" (Ps. 140:12). Praise God, Believers can win!

In general the Old Testament has something to say about the future hope of the Believer. In the Exodus God redeemed Israel on "eagles wings" (Exod. 19:4; Rev. 12:14). God has the "arrow of victory" powerful enough to defeat all enemies (2 Kings 13:17). Isaiah wrote: "Yet those who wait (hope in) for the LORD will gain new strength; they will mount up with wings like eagles, they will run and not get tired, they will walk and not become weary" (40:31). God assured Israel that their enemies would not "overcome" them because He was there to deliver in the present time and ultimately in Christ (2:10; Jer. 1:19; Dan. 2:44; 1 Cor. 15:57). Those who follow God will prevail over the enemy. God's people are never defeated!

The book of Revelation harmonizes with the entire Old Testament. It finishes the story of the ultimate victory of God's people, through Christ, that began in the Old Testament. Victory in Christ is not a subject that began in Revelation. It is a theme running through the Old and New Testaments. Victory in the Testaments is associated with the concepts of power, majesty, and the ability to prevail. These concepts are closely related to the word *nikao,* which describes Christ's ability to redeem, deliver, prevail, or overcome in the book of Revelation. The Old Testament uses three words for victory: (1) *yasha,* meaning to give ease or security (Ps. 98:1); (2) *netsach,* denoting prominence and pre-eminence; and (3) *teshuah,* which also means ease or security (1 Chron. 29:11; Isa. 25:8). It is significant for you to see this theme in the entire Bible which began in Genesis 3:15: "I will put enmity between you and the woman, and between your seed and her seed; He shall bruise you on the head, and you shall bruise him on the heel." God had to crush Satan on the head in order to give the believer hope and victory in the future. This He did through Christ, the seed of woman (Gal. 3:16)!

The word for hope in the Old Testament is: (1) *batach,* meaning to be confident, to trust and lean on God in order to feel and be secure in the faith (Job 6:20; Ezek. 28:26); (2) *yachal,* which denotes to wait with hope and endurance (Ps. 31:24; 33:18, 22; 119:114; 147:11; Ezek. 13:6); (3) *qawa,* which means to wait with earnest expectation, to look for, and hope for (Gen. 49:18; Isa. 38:18; 40:31; Jer. 14:22); (4) and *hasa,* denoting to have hope and to take refuge in God (Prov. 14:32) (Meyers 500).

The message of the Old Testament rings clearly with assurance, confident expectation, and future hope ranging in degree from an ordinary desire felt with eager anticipation to a defining characteristic of those who seek eternal security in God and experience His grace. In the theological sense, hope is a virtue constitutive of the people of God, both Israel in the Old Testament and the church in the New Testament (Ibid). For example, Job spoke generally of his hopelessness without God in dealing with the strength of Leviathan or Satan (Job 7:6; 14:7; 17:15; 19:10; 41:1-9). However, in the end of all his earthly struggles, Job knew that God can do all things and not a one of His purposes are thwarted (Job 42:1-6). God, through mercy and grace, gives hope to His faithful children.

One of the great stories in the Old Testament to reveal future hope and victory for God's people is in the fulfilled promise of Isaac, the child of redemption, beginning in Genesis eighteen. It took faith in God for Abraham and Sarah to believe and trust God to give them a son to deliver the world from sin. In this promise all the nations of the earth would be spiritually blessed beyond measure. Isaac delivered the promise through Jacob who became the twelve tribes of Israel to redeem man. Kaminski gives a good conclusion of the importance of the promise made to Isaac. In the redemption of man the fulfillment of God's promises, in spite of Isaac's incompetence, is a way of revealing God's greatness. And most importantly, it is in the laughter evoked by Isaac that one finds the strength to believe, even when trust in God's promises seem absurd" (Bown 372). Those redeemed in the Old Testament era trusted God and won the victory over enemies.

God "defeated" David's enemies at Baal Perazim and He said, "As waters break out, God has broken out against my enemies by my hand" (1 Chron. 14:11). God literally saved David from his enemies (1 Chron. 18:6, 13). We can clearly see that victory belongs to God and his children (20:15; 1 Chron. ESV). Victory comes as a result of fighting with God, not against Him (2 Chron. 13:10, 12, 18). We rely upon Him daily! The flesh cannot prevail over the strength of God (2 Chron. 14:11; 16:8; Heb. 13:5-6). We can "completely prevail over enemies with "The Lord's arrow of victory" (2 Kings 13:17). Faith gives victory, peace, comfort, and success (2 Chron. 20:20; Eph. 6:10-13). David said, "God will let me look in triumph on my enemies" (Ps. 59:10 ESV). David knew that he had victory because God has defeated "Leviathan" or Satan (6:9-10; Ps. 74:10-14; 104:26; 118:7). We can always call upon God in faith in order to succeed in the Christian life surrounded by enemies. Praise God, We Won!

FUTURE HOPE IN THE LIVING GOD

God is living and active in the lives of His people which is a great theme of the Old Testament. This is expressed in the Hebrew word *hay,* meaning alive or living, which occurs about 481 times in the Old Testament. Man in creation is a living being because he was created by a living God (Gen. 2:7). The living God also gave man the power to live, to overcome, to be healed, and to be redeemed. Man is helpless and hopeless without God!

Man alone cannot achieve hope and victory. It is accomplished by Divine power. God alone can conquer, is unconquerable, and makes man more than a conqueror through Jesus Christ. The story of victory that we can read about in the book of Revelation is a theme that began in the Old Testament. God works in the lives of His people through Christ who gives them victory over all enemies. Victory in the Old Testament is a Divine action, by the overthrow of an opposing force which is manifest to all humanity. One must first look to the Old Testament for the victory of God's people.

The people of God in the Old Testament wondered if mortals can ever finally achieve hope and victory over the struggles of life and their enemies. They asked two basic questions concerning the word *nikao*. Against this fundamental prerequisite, however, there are objections which are suggested by the realities of life and which are also reflected in the usage: a. Is the human eye sharp enough to discern between genuine and apparent victory? b. Can mortals ever finally achieve true victory (Kittel 4:942).

In the Septuagint (LXX) the verb *nikao* appears about ten times and the noun *nike* occurs about 25 times. The Hebrew word _nesah,_ related to these terms, means to have control of, endurance, strength, victory, perpetuity, preeminence, and future hope. God, the strength of Israel, is able to give victory over hostile powers to His people (1 Sam. 15:29; 1 Chron. 29:11). In Him the saints of God are more than conquerors. He is the One who delivers His people from their enemies (Gen. 14:19-20); our "shield" and "reward" (Gen. 15:1). God is the believer's hope, victory, and success! This is relevant to this writing because God is the real Victor through Jesus Christ.

Mortals can achieve true victory by following God's message in the Bible. The book of Revelation draws from the Old Testament, especially in books such as Daniel, Ezekiel, and Zechariah, to give man a true message of victory. Douglas and Tenney did a great work in tracing this general theme in the Bible:

The OT associates victory with the God of power and glory and majesty who is in full control of his creation (1 Chron. 29:11). That he gives victory in this life to faithful believers is seen throughout Hebrews 11. Faith is the victory that conquers the world (1 John 5:45), and through it Christians continually know the victory because of what God has done in Jesus Christ (1 Cor. 15:7). They can look unafraid at the vanquishing of sin and death – and they will not suffer the second death (Rev. 2:11). All the blessings of the New Testament will be inherited by the over comers (1050).

Future hope in the Old Testament is always directed toward the presence and power of God in overcoming sin and worldly power (Ps. 65:5; 71:5). God is the "hope and Savior of Israel in time of distress (trouble)" prevailing over all adversaries and oppression (Jer. 14:8; Isa. 43:3; Ps. 9:9). Israel had future hope in God for their salvation as seen in the following:

Israel had a general desire and hope for personal salvation (Ps. 119:166) and corporate salvation (Jer. 29:11; 31:17). The means whereby hope is inspired in the people's heart is God's word, the center of which is the covenant (Ps. 119:43; 130:5). Because of his love, God has established himself as the hope of Israel through covenants with his people. God's pledge of himself and of his blessing is at the center of Old Testament hope. Israel, especially in the Monarchy, had shaped its hopes in accordance with what it conceived as the concrete fulfillment of God's promises. These expectations were shattered in the Exile (Ezek. 37:11), and while the hope of restoration to the land of promise continued, the prophets began to emphasize the expectation of a Messiah who would redeem his people. Israel's true situation, as the prophets realized, is summed up in the curious phrase "prisoners of hope" (Zech. 9:12), for even in the midst of captivity to their own folly and to foreign conquerors-God's people endure in the hope of salvation "because of the blood of my covenant with you" (v. 11) (Meyers 500).

Believers glorify God because He has the majesty, the power, the glory, and the victory over Satan in the heavens and on the earth (1 Chron. 29:11 NASU). The word "victory" (29:11) is the Hebrew word *netsach*, which means to have the preeminence. God has the preeminence in the lives of His people and over the world in which they live. For example, He has "swallowed up death forever" and "will wipe away all tears from off all faces" for His faithful people (Isa. 25:8). This is the victory you must see in the Old and New Testaments. He gives this victory to the faithful through Jesus Christ.

In connection with future hope and victory in God, one must realize the full meaning of the other word used in the Old Testament that expresses hope and victory, which is *yakol,* meaning to be able to endure and to prevail. It is used about two hundred times in the Old Testament. It first occurs in Genesis 13:6 when God told Abraham and Lot that the land of Canaan was not able to bear them. God later told Abraham that he would be able to number his seed as the stars of heaven (Gen. 13:16; 15:5). The seed promise was fulfilled in Jesus Christ who will ultimately prevail over all things in heaven and on earth (6:2; Gal. 3:16). In the negative sense, *yakol* presented a prohibition and a social barrier to fellowship with God and man because of sin (Gen. 43:32; Deut. 12:17). In the Book of Joshua the word referred to the one who had the moral ability to prevail over his enemies when he removed the accursed thing from among the people of God (Josh. 7:13). In the lives of Moses, David, and Daniel the word refers to the ability of God to deliver them when sin was removed from their lives (1 Sam. 17:33; Dan. 3:17). Sin has no victory!

41

The fact is of a certainty that the Old Testament provides the background of Revelation. The writings of Ezekiel and Daniel are undoubtedly two of the main sources of a similar type of imagery. The writer of the Apocalypse frequently used references from the Pentateuch, the Psalms, Isaiah, Ezekiel, and Zechariah, with the Book of Daniel yielding the greatest number. For example, the vision of Christ, the Son of Man, in the midst of the seven churches of Asia Minor, (1:13-3:22) is similar to Daniel's visions concerning the fall of Babylon (Dan. 7). The throne scene in heaven and the sealed book (4:1-5:14) rests on Ezekiel's vision of the glory of God over the cherubim (Ezek. 10). The vision of the four horsemen coming forth to conquer (6:18) takes its background from Zechariah's vision of the victory and comfort God gave to Jerusalem over her enemies (Zech. 4).

The Old Testament assured God's people of victory in various areas of life based upon certain requirements. First, they had to be among God's chosen people or "of the seed of the Jews" (Esth. 6:13; Exod. 19:56). Mordecai prevailed against Haman because he was of the seed of God's people. The victorious Christ gives victory to those who are called, chosen, and faithful (17:14). This is the heart of the visions of victory in Revelation. Second, man in the Old Testament could not prevail with his own strength and holiness (1 Sam. 2:9; Ps. 9:19). He had to put away wickedness and be holy as God is holy. He must be free from sin to be holy just as the blood of Christ frees man from sin in the Revelation (1:5). Third, God blessed those who did mighty works (1Sam. 26:25). David was blessed without measure over Saul because he did God's commandments. The book of Revelation stresses the significance of doing God's commandments in works of obedience (1:3; 7:14-15; 14:12; 22:14). Fourth, all of this is summed up in Israel's willingness to rely upon God and prevail (2 Chron.13:18; 14:11-12). Wicked men did not prevail over the children of Judah because they relied upon the strength of God. Jesus Christ came through the tribe of Judah to give victory to those who rely upon God in obedience to his word (5:5; 17:14). In many areas of life the people who did these things were blessed. In all the following areas of victory one must remember that the "victory is of Jehovah"

(Prov. 21:31). Victory comes with the wisdom of God (Prov. 24:6). The righteous will "triumph" over sin and worldliness (Prov. 28:12). Praise God, we won!

VICTORY OVER ENEMIES

The people of God in the Old Testament prevailed over their enemies. The Israelites won many battles with their enemies because the hand of God was with them (Exod. 17:8, 11). Moses took "the rod of God" with him to the mountain, while Israel fought Amalek and prevailed in battle. God led his people to victory during the days of the Judges in Israel, when they prevailed over many of their enemies in Canaan (Num. 22:6). One of these great battles was during the reign of Othniel who was "a savior to the children of Israel" (Judg. 3:7-11). The "Spirit of Jehovah" delivered "Mesopotamia" into the hand of Othniel and he prevailed against "Cushanrishathaim" (Judg. 3:11). David led the children of Israel to victory over the Philistines. He prevailed with the hand of God (1 Sam. 17:46-50). David encouraged Israel to praise God for giving victory and dominion to them over all their enemies (Ps. 18:1-3; 89:10; 68:1). God delivered Syria through "a great and honorable man" like Naaman (2 Kings 5:1f). God always won the victory. Israel had future hope in God!

Through the writings of prophets like Isaiah and Daniel, we are told of the coming Messiah, who is the Christ that would bring the ultimate victory over the enemies of the people of God. It is a beautiful study to note these with their New Testament fulfillment in Jesus Christ. Isaiah said he would "come forth a shoot out of the stock of Jesse" and "recover the remnant of his people" (Isa. 4:2; 11:1, 11). Jesus Christ came out of the seed of David, the root of Jesse, to give the ultimate hope and victory to the people of God (5:5; Acts 13:22-23). He would have the "Spirit of Jehovah" through great wisdom, understanding, counsel, power, knowledge, and reverence for God (Isa. 11:2). He would judge the people with righteousness and faithfulness (Isa. 11:35; John 5:22, 30). He would bring peace and justice to the land (Isa. 11:6-16; Eph. 2:13-17). Theologically speaking, the Old Testament is filled with future hope and victory in Christ. Victory is a theological theme in this first text God gave His people. Today, Believers are encouraged to accept this assurance over all enemies.

VICTORY IN THE KINGDOM OF GOD

In the Old Testament one is told of the hope and victory in the Kingdom of God. The word kingdom basically comes into the Hebrew in the words *malekuth* and *mamlakah.* The word *malekuth* first appears in the prophecy of Balaam as he blessed the kingdom of Israel (Num. 24:7). It refers "to the kingdom, rule, and reign of God. *Malekuth* comes into the Septuagint in the word *basileia* which means kingship, kingdom, and royal power" (Vine 129). The rule of David was the theocratic system that God used to rule over His people and give them hope, blessing, and victory. In David God established His kingdom of spiritual blessing with His people forever (2 Sam. 7:16). The term 'kingdom' to the Jews meant deliverance, hope, victory, and the presence of a sovereign God. Therefore, humanity is under the rule of God. Hope and victory is the result of God ruling the universe. Consequently, the Old Testament fully and completely recognizes hope for the world in the kingship of God.

The climax of Balaam's prophecy in Numbers 24 is the "star" coming out of Jacob to exalt the kingdom of God and have dominion over all nations. The general understanding of the Hebrew people was the rule of God in defeating Moab by Amalek under David (2 Sam. 7:16). Today, as one makes an application of future hope from the Old Testament, the ultimate victory was culminated in Jesus Christ, the Bright and Morning Star, who defeated the sins of Jerusalem (AD 70) and finally Rome (2:28; 22:16; Matt. 2:2). Burton Coffman gives some good reasons why this prophecy should be interpreted first during the rule of David with a secondary application to Jesus Christ:

> Even in the dim light of pre-Christian gloom the writers of the Dead Sea Scrolls enthusiastically

44

accepted the Messianic import of this chapter. Also, the Jewish scholars of all ages read the passage as a promise of the blessed Messiah. The proof of this lies in the behavior of a false messiah, Bar Kochba, who led a Jewish revolt against Rome (132-133 B.C.). The name assumed by this impostor was "Bar Kochba", meaning "Son of the Star" (Coffman 477).

The Old Testament also uses the word *malekuth* in the book of Esther to denote four things significant to the hope and victory of God's people: (1) the territory of the glorious kingdom which God showed to Esther (Esth. 1:4; (2) the accession to the throne and deliverance of the Jews under Esther (4:14); (3) the year of Esther's reign (2:16); (4) anything "royal" or "kingly": throne (Esth. 1:2), wine (1:7), crown (1:11), word (1:19), garment (6:8), palace (1:9), scepter (Ps. 45:6), and glory (Ps. 145:11-12) (Vine 129). God gave His people hope of future deliverance each time they were taken into captivity and finally saved them through Jesus Christ.

ESCHATOLOGICAL HOPE AND VICTORY

God gave victory in Jewish eschatology. Eschatology is a study of last things. These things were promised in the Old Testament and fulfilled in the New Testament. The children of Israel sang the victory song because with God's help they had "triumphed gloriously" over Egypt (Exod.15:1f). This powerful nation, fierce as a many headed dragon such as the "sea monsters" by the Nile and the "Leviathan" (Ps. 74:13-14), was destroyed to deliver Israel, who otherwise was hopelessly trapped at the Red Sea. The song of Moses, telling of the strength, loving-kindness, and salvation of God over all their enemies, was echoed in the celebration song in Revelation concerning the Christian's final salvation in heaven (15:14). God, the King of Israel, led his people to victory in battle on earth and in heaven (Num. 21:16; Ps. 24:8). He is the King of kings to whom all kings and gods must pay final homage (Ps. 95:3; 96:4). Jesus Christ is King of kings to whom all men and gods must pay final homage (17:14). The book of Revelation has a rich background in the Old Testament with its theme that God has the ultimate victory in the lives of his people. The greatest enemy of God's people since the Garden of Eden experience has always been Satan! However, Believers have hope of deliverance through the presence and power of God.

In things pertaining to death and salvation, God was a refuge to the children of Israel (Ps. 46; 48; 98:1). God swallowed up death in victory (Isa. 25:8; 1 Cor. 15:57). In these eschatological events, the sovereignty of God gave comfort and hope of deliverance to Israel (1 Chron. 29:11; 2 Chron. 13:5). Men like Moses, Joshua, Othneil, and David were saviors to Israel. Isaiah, Jeremiah, Daniel, and Ezekiel showed both the hope and the final victory of God's people. Jeremiah lived in an age much like the people of God in the book of Revelation. He kept calling for renewal of the people's covenant with God and pointed the people to the "balm in Gilead", which was culminated in the Great Physician, Jesus Christ (6:10; Jer. 8:21, 22; Matt. 9:10-13). The people of God were led to victory over sin, oppression, their enemies, and death. There were many prophecies given of the victory of the Messiah, Jesus Christ, and His kingdom which were fulfilled in the New Testament. Jesus Christ is the victorious Savior of the New Testament. He will deliver his people to the ultimate victory in heaven like the men of the Old Testament led God's people to victory on earth. Praise God, we win!

There is great messianic hope in the Old Testament. Jesus Christ's fulfilling prophecy brought the hope and victory of the Old Testament to fruition. One must have faith in God's ability to deliver those who cry for help through Jesus Christ (6:10; Ps.140:12). He came out of the tribe of Judah, the Root of David, to open the message of victory to those suffering persecution (5:5). The saved will sing the victory song of glory and honor to his dominion forever at the throne of God in heaven (5: 9, 13).

HOPE OF IMMORTALITY

The Old Testament says little about life after death or immortality which relates to the study of last things. It uses the term "Sheol", or the netherworld, some 66 times in reference to life after death. Job asked the question, "If a man dies, will he live again? All the days of my struggle I will wait until my change comes" (Job 14:14). Job may have had a dim conception of life after death, but he stated some belief in it with anticipating the change. The prophet Isaiah taught that "Sheol is excited to meet the spirits" of the dead (14:9). Daniel taught that those in Sheol will resurrect to "everlasting life" (12:1-2). Therefore, the Jews in the Old Testament period had an understanding of life after death or immortality.

What did the people of the ancient world such as Ugarit, a region of the ancient Mediterranean West Asia, believe about death and life thereafter? It was not the Judeo-Christian belief in a blessed physical afterlife, but it did meet with the reality of death. Schmidt's research reveals the faith in Sheol:

> In addition to the belief that the dead persisted physically in some weakened, shadowy form in the netherworld, they instituted cults of commemoration (or what anthropologists like the British Africanist Meyers Fortes refer to as geneonymy). Commemorative cults were and are designed to generate and sustain the recollection of the deceased in the minds of the living – those of both family and community. They have as their impetus the compulsion to avoid having to suffer the dreaded "death after death" or relegation of one's deeds or personhood to eternal anonymity (Hesse 237-8).

King David believed in Sheol as a place of peace (1 Kings 2:6, 9). Isaiah taught the reality of Sheol which would be connected to the coming of Immanuel or the Christ (Isaiah 7:11; Matt. 1:23; Luke

16:19-31). Christ believed and taught the reality of Sheol as a place of punishment for the wicked and peace for the righteous. The Old Testament word "Sheol" has two significant meanings as noted by W. E. Vine:

> First, the word means the state of death: "For in death there is no remembrance of thee: in the grave who shall give thee thanks?" (Ps. 6:5; Cf. 18:5). It is the final resting place of all men: "They spend their days in wealth, and in a moment go down to the grave (Job 21:13). Hannah confessed that it was the omnipotent God who brings men to sheol (death) or kills them (1 Samuel 2:6). Second, "Sheol" is used of a place of conscious existence after death. In the first biblical appearance of the word of Jacob said that he would "go down into the grave unto my son mourning" (Gen. 37:35). All men go to "Sheol" – a place and state of consciousness after death (Ps. 16:10); the wicked receive punishment (Num. 16:30; Deut. 32:22), and it is a refuge and reward for the righteous (227).

The people of God look to the relationship of death in three stages: First, they expected a deliverance from death because of their relationship to God as the Ruler (Ps. 18:4-5; 88:4-12; 1 Sam. 2:6). They realized that they must die, but God resurrects them to life (Deuteronomy 32:39). Second, they looked to the experience of transcendence through the participation of eternal life beyond the physical realm (Job 19:25-27; 2 Kings 2). The Hebrews believed they would dwell in the house of the Lord eternally (Ps. 23). Third, the faith of the Bible, its hope and expectation encompasses the resurrection of the dead to a new world of life everlasting (Daniel 12:1-2). The resurrection was brought to a reality through the death, burial, and resurrection of Christ (Matt. 28:1-6; 2 Tim. 1:10). The Gospel of Christ tells the story accurately for the Believer today.

FUTURE HOPE IN THE MESSAGE OF THE PROPHETS

Believers, as in the Old Testament, must not forfeit their future hope and victory by committing sin. For example, the future hope of Israel of the Promised Land was jeopardized by sin, especially sexual sins (House 143-44). God is the One who saves His people according to Isaiah, the Messianic Prophet (Isa. 53). Jeremiah proclaimed that God enforces the covenant. God reveals Himself through these suffering prophets to Israel as the Redeemer. This is helpful for one to understand the suffering due to the ministry and the Christian life. Isaiah was the prophet that stands out to this author as the one who predicted the future hope of Israel in the Messiah. Ezekiel presents the comfort of the Divine Presence to instruct and comfort the exiles.

The people of God in Israel trampled underfoot their enemies with God's help. Isaiah wrote: "Who stirred up one from the east whom victory meets at every step? He gives up nations before him, so that he tramples kings underfoot; he makes them like dust with his sword, like driven stubble with his bow" (41:2 ESV). God will deliver the faithful. God will not allow His people to be defeated!

House fits five theological themes into Isaiah, Jeremiah, and Ezekiel, as well as stating that, as a group, the latter Prophets provide the canon with an interpretation of the history that has already been described in the Law and the Former Prophets. He wrote:

> The Sovereignty of God in giving eternal life
> God's presence to correct and instruct to have eternal life.
> The eternal nature of the Davidic Kingdom.
> God dealing with the sins of mankind.
> The reality of the mercy and grace of God to forgive those who repent (273).

Jeremiah lived in an age much like our own. While the kings of Judah adopted the ill-fated politics of shifting alliances with

49

various power blocks, Jeremiah kept calling for internal renewal of the people's covenant with God. His preaching was not the bitter denunciation of a turncoat, but the heart broken pleadings of a man who could say, "My heart has been crushed because my people are crushed." He asked, "Is there no medicine in Gilead?" Yes, there were doctors of faith in Israel (Jer. 8:21, 22). God brought victory to His people, even demanding the rights of the foreigner (Lev. 19:33, 34). God has supremacy over all powers (Deut. 10:17-19). God has a plan of "hope" for our "future" (Jer. 29:11). The only hope our world has is victory through the power of God!

In the Latter Prophets (12 books) the message magnifies, defines, and describes the transgressions; to threaten their punishment; to anticipate their chastisement which is coming later; then to end with restoration back to God preparing for eternity. House makes a victory statement of the future of Israel's hope by saying that just as Ezekiel looks beyond punishment to a brighter future based on God's presence in the remnant's midst, so Haggai, Zechariah, and Malachi point toward God's eventual transformation of judgment to glory (Ibid).

In this respect all the prophets tie the message together to present a brighter future hope for the children of Israel. Today, we must look beyond the punishment and the misfortune of the world to see the hope of a much brighter future to the glory of God!

THE GOD OF VICTORY

The Old Testament declares there is a God in heaven who desires His people to have the future hope of victory in life and finally salvation. The entire world must know and love the God of heaven. It is wonderful to live in a country that is allowed to love, serve, follow, and worship God. He is wonderful, the Mighty God and everlasting Father of Israel and the church (Isa. 9:6). This was ultimately fulfilled in Jesus Christ (Luke 2:11; John 3:16; Matt. 28:18). The story of the Old Testament is we win in Christ!

How do you define God? It is difficult to give a full, complete, and perfect definition of the one unique Supreme Being in the entire universe. What better terminology could be used than the words "I AM" that Moses used to describe God in the deliverance of Israel from the Egyptian bondage (Exod. 3:10-15). God gave Israel hope of deliverance through His sovereign power exercised through Moses. God is the Supreme Personal Spirit of the universe who is in complete control. He is the source, support, and end of the universe (Gen. 1:1-2). He is a Person, not a glorified 'It', who loves and cares for His people, promising hope in all generations. He is the Absolute and Perfect Personality who transcends the world (Eph. 4:6). He is very much present in all generations to give hope and victory!

What does it mean for God to be personal? He is a personal, self-conscious, and rational Being, who is very loving, caring, and compassionate toward man. Many deny this attribute of God, but He is everywhere present in both the Old and New Testaments. However, the Bible is in full support of the fact that God exists and is personally involved in the lives of His people, giving them future hope of deliverance from a world of sin. What makes God a personal being, the One to supply hope? Hope serves you until it ends in reality-heaven.

GOD IS ALIVE! Believers serve the true and living God. The living God fulfilled His promise of the hope of deliverance over all enemies in the words of Joshua: "Then Joshua said to the sons of Israel, `Come here, and hear the words of the Lord your God.' Joshua said, `By this you shall know that the living God is among you, and that He will assuredly dispossess from before you the Canaanite, the Hittite, the Hivite, the Perizzite, the Girgashite, the Amorite, and the Jebusite" (Josh. 3:9-10). One must note that this promise of hope is based upon obedience to the word of God. In the New Testament Paul wrote: "For they themselves report what kind of a reception you gave us. They tell how you turned to God from idols to serve the living and true God" (1 Thess. 1:9). This promise of hope is based upon repentance of idolatry. There is beyond the azure blue, a living and true God, concealed from human sight, but who gives to all life and breath with eternal hope (Acts 17:28). The person and being of man comes from God who is very much alive (Gen. 2:7). God causes man to live victoriously.

GOD IS A REAL LIVING PERSONALITY! He is not a glorified "It." He is not an impersonal force in the universe. He is an all-powerful personality who delivers all believers (Gen. 17:1; Matt. 28:19-20). He is intelligent, self-conscious, self-determining, and moral, capable of saving His people. He is the perfect personality who rules the universe (Matthew 5:48). God is personal! He transcends the earth and all things therein, including humanity.

GOD IS LOVE! Man is a person who can love because God is love. The Old Testament is full of teaching on the love of God. Isaiah wrote: "In all their distress he too was distressed, and the angel of his presence saved them. In his love and mercy he redeemed them; and he lifted them, and carried them all the days of old" (63:9). God always saw the afflictions of Israel and responded with love and mercy in redemption. John, the apostle of love wrote: Dear friends, let us love one another, for love comes from God. Everyone who loves has been born of God and knows God. Whoever does not love does not know God, because God is love. "Dear friends, since God so loved us, we also ought to love one another" (1 John 4:7, 8, 11). We are manifest in his sight to receive the hope of redemption (Heb. 4:13). The death of Christ on the cross demonstrates the love of God for sinners (Rom. 5:8). The love of God was manifested in our lives by the Holy Spirit following the death and resurrection of Christ.

GOD CARES FOR MAN! God had an anxious care for Israel in Exile which is demonstrated in the message of the book of Ezekiel. Therefore, believers can cast all their care upon Him because He truly cares for them in the struggles of life (1 Pet. 5:7). David knew that God would bring down to Sheol the treacherous and the enemies of Israel. He wrote: "Cast your cares on the LORD and He will sustain you; He will never allow the righteous to fall. But you, O God, will bring down the wicked into the pit of corruption; bloodthirsty and deceitful men will not live out half their days. But as for me, I will trust in You" (Ps. 55:22-23). Our hope and trust must be in God who delivers from all enemies! God cares when His children hurt and suffer. Will you completely trust Him for such hope?

It is great to serve the true and living God of hope and victory. God is living among His people. He is God, the Father, the Son, and the Holy Spirit who rules the universe. He cares for man now and in eternity! I intend to share a message of victory in Christ from a survey of the literature in the Old Testament. God gave this great Book to assure Believers the power to overcome despite earthly circumstance. God, Christ, and the Holy Spirit are the 'awesome' ruling the universe. Why worry?

Chapter 3

Victory In The New Testament

The New Testament harmonizes with the Old Testament to tell one story of the victory of God's people. Victory in Christ is the beautiful theme of the New Testament, especially the book of Revelation. Many things have already been mentioned about this victory; however, there are other points of victory yet remaining worthy of attention.

The New Testament usage of the word "overcome" (5:5) describes the victory Christ has in conflict with opposing forces in the spiritual sense. It appears in the Gospels, the Epistles, and most frequently in the Revelation. It describes the Christian who is victorious in spiritual conflict for the cause of Christ (3:21b; 5:5; 6:2). Satan is conquered by Christians through the blood of Christ (12:11). The word *nikos* describes the means Christians have for being victorious (2:7, 11, 17, 26; 3:5, 12, 21; 21:7). That means faith in Christ (1 John 5:4). The noun *nike* is used to describe the power Christ has to confer victory on the Christian (1 Cor. 15:57). Jesus Christ is the God of victory for Believers as opposed to the Greek goddess *Nike*, who was a symbol of personal superiority in Rome (1:8). We are superior in Christ.

THE GOSPELS

The word "victory" appears twice in the Gospels. The first usage is in Matthew's account of the first Servant Song (Isa. 42:14) describing the victory of Christ in bringing justice to the Gentiles (Matt. 12:20). There are two parallel accounts in the Gospels of Jesus overcoming "the strong man" and giving his followers complete victory (Matt. 12:29; Mark 3:27; Luke 11:22). Jesus identifies Satan as the strong man (Matt. 12:26-29). The story of the final victory over Satan, the supreme enemy of man, is told in the Apocalypse (20:1f). Christ has complete victory in the "kingdom" which will always stand against Satan (1:6, 9; Matt. 12:25-26; 16:18-19). He gives victory over sin in rendering to man complete forgiveness (1:5; 7:14; Matt. 12:31). Finally, Jesus controls the world as it exists now and the world to come (21:1f; Matt. 12:32). Jesus Christ is God's chosen servant who came to this world to give hope and victory to both Jews and Gentiles (1:5; 17:14; Matt. 12:18, 21; 20:28). He is the true Victor!

The Jewish idea of the Messiah, the Son of David, was that of a restorer of Israel and a deliverer of the Gentiles to God's presence. It was understood that salvation would come through the restoration of David's throne and kingdom on earth (20:1-6; Isa. 26-27; Matt. 20:20-28; Acts 1:6-8). They thought the Messiah would be a martial conqueror. The word 'kingdom', from Matthew 12:26, 28 and Mark 10:35, depicts the Jewish idea that Christ was more of a military and political, rather than a religious, leader, which is contrary to his commission as conqueror of Satan. It is evident from both Jewish and Christian sources that popular messianism is of the warlike type. "The Messiah is primarily the great conqueror and national hero, appointed by God as his instrument for the destruction of the Gentiles and the liberation of Israel (cf. Ps. Sal. 17:21ff; Iv Ezra 11-13, etc.)" (Leivstad 7-8).

Jesus Christ defeated the Jews in their zelotic messianism. He came to defeat organized religion by starting a Revolution called Christianity. He came to defeat Satan in every avenue of the flesh, which wars against man's spiritually (Matt. 4:1-11). He refused the portrait of a political, militant deliverer (Luke 2:34; John 18:36). He brought spiritual peace to those who traditionally thought only in terms of an earthly messianic kingdom (Matt. 10:34f). He gave many words of doom and punishment to these wicked and rebellious Jews by teaching against their traditions (Luke 11:49f; 19:27, 41f). The destruction of Jerusalem was a consequence of Israel's rejection of Jesus, the Messiah (Matt. 21:41, 43; 23:37; 24:1f). Jesus is described as a successful Savior of man lost in sin (Mark 13:20, 26-27). He was not a proud, earthly conqueror riding a restless war horse, but a Prince of Peace dressed in humility, riding the colt of a donkey (Mark 11:1f) and a white horse representing a spiritual war of purity and righteousness in conflict with sin (6:2; 19:1f). He marches before in all power and victory.

The Gospels and the book of Revelation agree that Christ came to disarm and despoil the power of Satan. In the Gospels he is binding Satan, the strong man (Matt. 12). In the Revelation he has the final victory over Satan (Rev. 20). The metaphorical meaning of the word victory, *nikao,* is the binding of Satan. The metaphor explains Jesus' superiority over the demonic powers. "If it is by the finger of God that I cast out demons, then the kingdom of God has come upon you" (Luke 11:20). "The earthly Jesus demonstrates by His actions that He is the hidden victor over the forces opposed to God, whilst it is not until the resurrection that He achieves the final victory over sin, death, and the devil" (Colin Brown 1:651).

The second use of the word victory is in the Gospel of John (16:33). John uses the word 'world', *kosmos,* to reveal the victory Christ has over the forces opposed to God. Jesus came to earth, died on the cross, and returned to the Father to win victory over the world. John uses the perfect tense of *nikao* to express this victory. The perfect tense indicates a completed action with continuing results. God has already determined this victory. Thus, victory is described in the power Christ has to limit the activity of Satan in the world. Satan, the ruler of this world, has had his power restricted by Jesus Christ. That is, Jesus, as the stronger man, has freed His people from the power of the evil One. The battle has thus been decided by God. By faith Christians participate in this victory and are thus placed in a position to overcome the world. Faith is the victory over the world (1 John 5:4).

Jesus assured the disciples of victory over Satan and the world. He had almost completed His mission into the world and was so certain of its completion that He spoke of it as a reality. Believers overcome the allurements and temptations of the world by an obedient faith in the Lord Jesus Christ. He won the initial triumph of salvation on the cross. He entered the world and bound the strong man (Satan) at the cross and gave man a means of victory over sin in the world (Col. 2:14-15). We must stop looking and loving the world through rose-colored glasses and love Jesus, looking to Him for victory over sin and the world! We should eagerly acknowledge this victory which was decided in heaven.

THE EPISTLES

The great story of victory in the New Testament Epistles is triumph in Jesus Christ over Satan, the world, sin, and death. The center of this victory is spoken most forcibly by Paul in Romans 8 and I Corinthians 15. The heart of the matter is in the redemptive work of Christ in making Believers "more than conquerors" (6:2; Rom. 8:34-37). Believers have this blessing because of Christ's death and resurrection (1 Cor. 15:57). They cannot be separated from the love of Christ by "tribulation, anguish, persecution, famine, nakedness, peril or sword" (Rom. 8:35). The world, the cosmic powers, and death have lost their controlling power in the life of a Christian (2 Cor. 4:7f). The ruler of this world has no victory because of the death and resurrection of Christ!

The Epistles give a background to the victory that Christ would give the church over Satan, the world (which included the Roman Empire), sin, and death. The core teaching of the Epistles is salvation in Christ who defeats Satan. John wrote of the final defeat of all these enemies in the Revelation of Jesus Christ.

Satan is the great opponent of those who are called out of the world by Jesus Christ. Satan is the great tempter, seducing the people of God to commit sin and apostasy. Christ opposes Belial, the wicked one (2 Cor. 6:15). Christ and Belial represent two opposite realms. Christ represents the realm of light, righteousness and the believers in the temple of God (2 Cor. 6:16f.). Belial represents darkness, sin, and the idols of unbelievers. He personifies the impure worship of the cult of Aphrodite, the Greek goddess of love and beauty. Aphrodite is identified in the Roman world with Venus. Paul predicted that Satan, the serpent, the destroyer, and the god of this world, would be crushed by Christ (Rom. 16:20). This ultimate victory is seen by John in the Apocalypse.

Paul refers to apocalyptic ideas in at least one passage (2 Thess. 2:1-12). The lawless one, the antichrist, persecutes the church with his immoral and blasphemous behavior. "Paul's writing is parallel to the rise and fall of the Roman Empire which is described in Revelation 13 in four ways. (1) The "man of sin" opposes everything that is authorized by God in deceiving the world through false prophecy, performing miracles and signs, and usurping the Messiah (13:6; 2 Thess. 2:3-4a). (2) He is worshipped calling himself God which is going on at the time of the writing of Paul and John (AD 53-96) (13:8, 12; 2 Thess. 2:4b, 7). (3) Christ is the one who will slay the "man of sin" with the sword of his mouth, which is the word of God (2:16; 17:9-14; 19:5; 2 Thess. 2:8). (4) The coming of the "lawless one" is according to the work of Satan (13:2; 2 Thess. 2:9-12). Domitian (AD 52-96) succeeded Nero in bringing a cruel persecution against Christians in his hatred and hostility to God. He enforced the worship of Nero, calling himself "Lord and God" (M'Clintock and Strong 2:860).

The world of sin, death, and the flesh, with all its demonic powers, is defeated in Christ. Satan is the cause of sin and death in the world (Gen. 3). He is the prince, or ruler, of this world of sin and death. These are caused by the disobedient following the lust of the eyes, the flesh, and the pride of life (1 John 2:15-17). The rudiments or elements of the world such as sin, angelic worship, authority of Satan, and death, are defeated in obedience to Jesus Christ (Col. 2:8-23). Christ removed the fear of death in delivering man from sin (Rom. 5:12-17; Heb. 2:13-16). Death has no holding power to those in Christ (2 Tim.

1:10). Believers have the ultimate victory. The book of Revelation is easier to understand with the background of the Epistles. Victory in Christ is seen throughout the New Testament.

THE REVELATION

The victory of God's children began with the prediction of Christ in the Old Testament. It is sealed with the coming of Christ in the Gospels, detailed in the Epistles, and culminated in Revelation. In Revelation 2 and 3, Christ sent seven letters to the churches of Asia Minor with a call to overcome persecution caused by Satan, sin, the world, and death. These worldly persecutions are not final. The foundations for victory have been laid by Jesus Christ. He has already won the victory. The ultimate promise of victory is given in the inheritance of the Victor (21:7). We inherit our Father's victory through Christ.

In the book of Revelation, some Believers are depicted as having followed God through Christ in the conflict against Satan pouring out their blood in martyrdom, thus winning the victory in heaven (6:2; 11:7; 13:7). The Lamb and his followers win and are seen standing on Mt. Zion singing a hymn of praise to the King of kings and Lord of lords (14:1; 15:2f; 17:14). The victory of the people of God is secure despite all confrontations with Satan and the world. Christians have victory in Christ over all enemies.

God assured His people victory in the Old Testament. Christ secured Believers with the power to win over all tribulation and personal enemies which includes Satan in the New Testament. In the following chapter, I intend to communicate a message of victory in a personal relationship with God through Christ, which is available to all Believers.

⫷ *Chapter 4* ⫸

Victory In Christ

Our thoughts of victory may disintegrate into a success that has us focus our attention on our accomplishments, almost to the exclusion of Christ. To talk of victory in John's terms in the Revelation is to speak of the victory by Christ and in Christ. To talk of victory without Christ is to talk of nonsense and defeat. He is the very source of true victory. Praise God for victory in Christ!

John, the apostle living among other Christians in Asia Minor, had never seen a leader like Jesus. The emperors in all their glory, pride, and boasts were never like this. John fell at his feet and heard the victorious words: "When I saw him, I fell at his feet as though dead. Then he placed his right hand on me and said: 'Do not be afraid. I am the First and the Last. I am the Living One; I was dead, and behold I am alive forever and ever! And I hold the keys of death and Hades'" (1:17-18).

The "No Fear" T-shirts are worn everywhere by young people. Yet, society is filled with precious people, young and old, who fear economic failure, natural disasters, the end of the world, death, and many other suchlike worries and concerns. The irony of all this is that many of these paranoid people come to my office with feelings of rejection, inferiority, hopelessness, and isolation, while wearing "No Fear" on their shirts. What a contradiction! Jesus died so we will have NO Fear! The great message in the Revelation of Jesus Christ to the church in every age is, "Fear not; I am the first and the last" (1:17). The word 'afraid' is the word 'fear', which is an unpleasant, often strong emotion caused by anticipation or awareness of danger. It is a state marked by this emotion or an anxious concern (2:10; 11:18; 14:7; 15:4; 19:5). It is often expressed in terms like DREAD, FRIGHT, ALARM, PANIC, TERROR, AND TREPIDATION, which mean painful agitation in the presence or anticipation of danger. FEAR is the most general term used in the New Testament and implies anxiety and usually loss of courage or *fear* of the unknown.

Jesus wants believers to have the positive side of fear, which means a profound reverence and awe especially toward God (cf. Acts 10:35). Society must come back to faith in Christ. He is alive and active in the lives of Believers by faith (Eph. 3:14-21). In Christ we have no fear of the unknown. He has explained the unknown to us in this book! We must read it with joy! Jesus Christ is our hero. God's desire for believers is security. He does not want us to serve Him out of fear. We must never be afraid of God. It is our heart's desire to enter heaven with joy! Praise God, we won!

The theme of Revelation is victory in Jesus Christ (17:14). The word 'overcome' will be studied in relationship to Jesus Christ, who will be victorious and conquer the enemies of Christianity (3:21b; 5:5). The word indicates that the Victor is able to give victory to Christians in the moral and religious sense. The message of Christ overcoming the dragon, through His spiritual kingdom, is completed with the message of victory in the book of Revelation (12:11-12; John 18:36). Jesus Christ gave the message of this book, having received it from God, to John, to show the servants in the church by using signs or symbols (1:13). Why did Christ use symbols to relay this powerful message? "The personal safety of both writer and reader was endangered if the persecutors understood the true meaning of the book. For this reason the message of the Apocalypse was written to conceal the message from the outsider and to reveal its message to the initiated" (Summers 5).

THE DEITY OF CHRIST

John uses several descriptive phrases to exalt the deity of Christ. Christ is victorious because He is God. It is important to show the deity of Christ because God is the source of all victory (6:10; 1 Chron. 29:11; 1 Cor. 15:57). These suffering saints asked God when He would "avenge" or vindicate their rights before their persecutors. God answered their cry in the redemption of Jesus Christ. The greater answer to this question will be given later. John is describing an act of God in delivering His saints, through the work of Christ. God is not asleep to the evil and injustice of the world. God hears the cry of those being persecuted (Exod. 2:23-25). God will protect them from falling into complete destruction (Ps. 12:5; Rom. 12:19). Believers have help to overcome trials in Jesus Christ!

The book of Revelation is a testimony that God controls the affairs of man in this life. He is the *pantokrator,* or Almighty God, who is in control of the whole universe (1:4, 8; 4:8; Isa. 9:6). The terms 'the Alpha and the Omega' describe the omnipresence of Christ to comfort the persecuted saints. The word 'Almighty' describes the all-powerful nature of Christ to deliver the saints. Jesus, the Almighty God, will give redemptive victory to the suffering saints, as He delivered a widow from an unjust judge (1:8; Luke 18:18). The judgments of Christ in the Revelation express His wrath out of love which has repentance as its goal (3:19). The deity of Christ is the source of victory in the following passages.

Jesus Christ is the "faithful witness" (1:5; 3:14). He is both faithful and a witness of the divine nature of the Godhead. He is the fulfillment of the seed of David, as God promised in the Old Testament (5:5; Ps. 89:35-37; Acts 2:25f). He is faithful, dependable, trustworthy, and reliable as a firsthand witness of God who never changes (1 Cor. 10:13; Heb. 13:8). He testifies to the church with firsthand knowledge of God's will in a message of victory. We are winning at the present time the Faithful Witness resides with us!

Christ is the "first begotten of the dead" (1:5). God is the only power that can resurrect the dead. The resurrection declared to the world that Jesus is the first begotten Son of God (Ps. 2:7; 89:27; Col. 1:15, 18; Heb. 1:5). Christ demonstrated this divine power in bringing a new order to the general resurrection, which gives man the ability to live eternally with immortality and incorruptibility (1 Cor. 15:53-57). The phrase does not mean that He was the first to be raised from the dead (Luke 7:14-15; John 11:41-44). It means He was the first one resurrected to die no more (Col. 1:18). He abolished the holding power of death in his resurrection (2 Tim. 1:10) and rendered it inactive for the Believer (Heb. 2:14-15). Death is the second greatest fear of man. In Christ this fear is defeated! Death is perceived as the gateway to eternal life!

The deity of Christ is seen in the image of the "ruler of the kings of the earth or King of kings" (1:5; 6:12; 17:14; 19:11-16). The word "ruler" means leader, prince, chief, originator, founder, and author. Christ rules the kings of the earth with all of the divine authority of which He is the originator (1:5; 17:14; 19:16; Matt. 28:18-20). The church or kingdom of Christ, which He founded, is victorious, not the earthly kings of Rome (1:6, 9; Matt. 16:18-19). He exercises greater power to rule than the Sanhedrin and the rulers of the synagogues did in the lives of the Jews (Matt. 9:18, 23; Luke 14:15). He has greater power through serving humanity than the lords of the Gentiles (Matt. 20:20-28). Jesus Christ rules the power behind the kings or leaders of the nations. He rules Satan, the prince of this world, through His death on the cross (John 12:31-33). Jesus Christ will defeat the prince of the "kingdom of the air" (Eph. 2:2, NIV). The word "air" is defined as the sphere where the inhabitants of the world live, and because of their rebellious and godless condition, it constitutes the seat of Satan's authority (Vine 894). Christ will consume this kingdom into the heavenly kingdom with the preaching of the Gospel!

The King of kings rides a white horse, conquering the world (6:12). The heavenly armies of Christ also ride white horses (19:11-

16). The white horse is a symbol of spiritual warfare in the Gospel age. The white color is a symbol of victory in spiritual purity which is given through Christ, the leader or prince of the church. I maintain that the rider of the white horse is Christ, for three reasons. First, God gave a crown (*stephanos*), or victor's wreath, which is a symbol of life, joy, reward, and triumph to the church (2:10; 3:11), the 24 elders (4:4, 10), and Christ (6:2; 9:7; 12:1; 14:14). *Stephanos* is distinguished from *diadema* only in that it refers to a royal crown worn by a ruler (19:12). Christ was given a *diadem* as a symbol of kingly or imperial dignity. Second, the word 'conquer' is *nikao,* which means to overcome, to prevail, or to have the victory as applied to Christ as King of kings (17:14). Third, the context of chapter 6 reveals that the kings, princes, and chief captains of the earth ask the mountains to hide them from the wrath of the Lamb, demonstrated by the four horsemen (6:12-17).

Jesus Christ, the Lamb of God, is worthy to open the sealed book which reveals the story of the four horses, and to receive the glory, honor, and power of the King of kings (5:59, 12; John 1:29). The symbol of the white horse would be easy to interpret by the first century church because a Roman general celebrated victory riding a white horse down the streets of Rome, followed by his armies and his captives. Christ is pictured, after His resurrection and ascension, riding a white horse and giving a message of victory to Christians over war, famine, and death caused by persecution.

The Christian doctrine of God exhibits God as absolutely transcendent, and God is seen in Jesus, who is sovereign in the suffering of believers. In Scripture the sovereignty and suffering of God meet in Christ, the Lamb of God. Our freedom is within God's power and honor, for the cross also speaks of judgment and the ultimate victory over the power of evil. God suffers with man through Christ. One contemporary theologian, who has seriously attempted to work out the meaning of divine suffering, is Nicholas Berdyaev. He is led in this direction by the conviction that only a God who suffers with man in the world is believable (981). God suffered with our struggles in this life, sending Jesus to die as the

Lamb of God on the cross (Heb. 4:15). The cross not only speaks of judgment and suffering of evil, but also of love and victory over the power of evil. The mystery of the sovereign God who suffers, yet is not defeated, can perhaps be only pictured and not explained except in the *Apocalypse*, chapter five, where a wounded Lamb sits on the throne of everlasting power and authority (Berdyaev 983). Praise God for victory over sin!

We are saved by the Lamb of God! The story is told of a man traveling in Norway, who went to see a church building in a certain town. Looking up toward the tower he saw a carved figure of a lamb. He inquired about it and they told him that, while they were constructing the building one day, a workman high upon a scaffold lost his balance and began to fall. His fellow workers knew that he would be killed, but he was hurt only slightly. How did this marvelous victory happen? Well, just as he fell, a flock of sheep was passing by. He fell among them as they crowded together and his body landed right on top of a lamb. The lamb was crushed to death, but the man was saved. In commemoration of his escape, he carved a figure of the lamb on the top of the church building. Christ is the Lamb of God slain from the foundation of the world on the old rugged cross, for your sins and mine. He died to save us! Does your heart swell with gratitude as you think of His sacrifice? Do you not love Jesus, too? What will you carve in life to commemorate the victory you have in Jesus?

The last attribute of Christ's deity is the title, 'the Son of God' (2:18). He identifies himself to the church as the infallible Son of God and assures her of his presence in using this title (Matt. 1:23). He is God in human flesh in order to reveal his divine will and to give them warning and instruction on how to be victors (Matt. 16:18-19). The piercing eyes like "a flame of fire" describe his glory and judgment like the God of the Old Testament (Ezek. 1:27; Mal. 3:2). The Hebrew letter teaches that Christ has penetrating vision to see the obedience and faithful works of the church (1:14; 2:19; Heb. 4:13). He has the infinite vision of God to see all things on the earth (Zech. 4:10).

Christ, the Son of God, with feet like refined brass, is strong and durable to defend the church (2:18b; 1:15). In the Old Testament, brass symbolized God's strength to deliver his people, such as the brazen walls built to fortify them against the kings of Judah (Jer. 1:18-19). John uses this imagery to show that Christ is able to crush all enemies of the church under his feet (1 Cor. 15:24; Eph. 1:22-23). Christ has a perfect understanding of the stressful conditions of the church and is qualified to speak words of judgment and encouragement, as he did in the seven letters. Because he is so endowed, the church must hear him (2:7, 11, 17, 29; 3:6, 13, 22). The glory of God came down in human flesh in the deity of Christ.

THE HUMANITY OF CHRIST

Jesus Christ, in human flesh after his ascension, was seen in the midst of the church (1:9-20). There was nothing that could quicken the hopes of the distressed Christians any more readily than the vision of the exalted and triumphant Christ. The humanity of Christ served the same purpose for John personally (1:9) because he was in the 'tribulation', which was a present reality, not a millennial future (1:9). John was in a physical and spiritual state of affliction, or distress, from outward circumstances, as described by the word 'tribulation'. This word will be dealt with thoroughly in the upcoming chapter on enemies. The Christians such as John, who was exiled on the isle of Patmos for his testimony of Christ and his Word (1:9b), endured pressure, afflictions, distress, straits, and other persecutions from the Romans.

John was commissioned by Christ to write the letters to the churches (1:10-11). He was "in the Spirit" while in great tribulation for the Lord, which means he was under God's influence, power, and inspiration while writing this book. Likewise, John was "in the Spirit" during the throne scene of chapter four, where he was allowed to see into heaven and receive a message from God (4:2). Therefore, he was able to send them this inspired message of hope and victory.

The Revelation is a beautiful story of Christ among his churches (1:12-15). He was "like unto a son of man" (1:13; 14:14), and he appeared to John in his humanity. Christ talked with John, as God talked with Ezekiel, to reveal this message in human terms and to manifest himself glorified (Ezek. 1:26-28). Jesus had predicted to John that one day he would be glorified as the Son of man (Jn. 13:31-32). John now sees the glorified Christ. The vision is similar to the one God gave Daniel in a message of victory, to reveal the strength of his everlasting kingdom (Dan. 7:13-14; 10:16-21). John could very easily recognize that this was the Lord, for he had a similar experience when Jesus prepared fish for the disciples after a night of fishing (John 21:1-14). This was the last time that Jesus appeared to John after his resurrection to assure the disciples of his presence in their lives. In like manner, Christ's manifestation to John assured the faithful that he was with them during their persecution.

Jesus Christ was seen wearing the clothing of a priest and king (1:13). He is High Priest over the church, to help them overcome the flesh (Matt. 4:1-11; John 2:15-17), sin (Rom. 6:23), and infirmities (Heb. 4:14-16). He can defeat any persecuting king or priest on earth (17:14). He wears the priest's garment as mediator (1:13b; 2 Tim. 2:5). He has the wisdom, purity, and holiness of a priest, as seen in the symbol of the white hair (1:14; Isa. 1:18; Dan. 7:9; Matt. 17:16). He has strength to guide the church through persecution (1:15; Rom. 5:6-8). Refined brass has had all the impurities burned out, leaving it strong and durable. They could endure because Jesus endured and had the victory over the flesh. He had a loud and clear voice of authority over all nations and people (1:15; 14:2; 19:6; Ezek. 43:2).

John writes of the resources and power of Christ's ministry among the churches (1:16-18). Jesus came in human form to serve man (Matt. 20:28). In this last book he tells the church not to fear because he is still alive to serve, protect, and deliver her from persecution (1:16-17, 20). Victory in Christ replaces fear with faith (1 Jn. 5:4; Rev. 20:8). Christ's face was like the "sun shining in full strength", which is also used by Matthew as a symbol of his Majesty during the transfiguration (Matt. 17:2), and he held the "seven stars" in his right hand, the hand of power. In the Old Testament the right hand symbolized the personal agency, action, and royal power of God (1 Sam. 5:11; 26:23; Ps. 110:1). John uses the term to show the ruling position of the Son of God who will judge the nations (1:16; Matt. 25:31-46) Therefore, He, not Rome, controlled their destiny.

The "sharp two-edged sword" came out of the mouth of Christ (1:16). The word of God is referred to in scripture as "the sword of the Spirit" (Eph. 6:17) and "sharper than any twoedged sword" (Heb. 4:12). Christ uses this symbol of the Word of God to give instruction, protection, encouragement, and warning of judgment to the church and her persecutors (2:12, 16; 19:15; Isa. 49:2; John 12:48). Therefore, he fulfilled his promise that he would always be present to instruct them in the way of salvation (Matt. 18:20; 28:18-20). He assured John that he had power over death and Hades and commissioned him to write the message of this book without fear (1:19-20).

CHRIST ON HIS THRONE

There was a story told about a believer who became very upset at God during the Vietnam War. He came to the local preacher for some counseling crying with much fear, saying, "If God is all-powerful and omnipresent, so loving and caring, WHERE was He the day my son died in the war?" The preacher in a moment of time replied, "The same place He was when His Son died on the cross!" He was on His throne. Yes, God is always present everywhere from His throne in heaven. We can look into the heavens and know that God is with us. He is not far away and untouchable. He cares! Yes, He does, for you and me! We must realize as John did, when he wrote Revelation chapter four, that without God nothing would hold. God is over all and present in our lives to make all things right! He is preparing us for the beautiful throne room in heaven which he describes completely in the coming chapters.

We must see God on His throne from the human side. An elementary teacher sent her little boys and girls home one night with the homework assignment to look at some television commercials and see if they could relate them to God in some way. When the children came in the next day, she nearly fainted. They said, "God is like Bayer Aspirin: He works wonders. God is like Dial soap: He gives you around the clock protection. God is like Ford: He has a better idea. God is like Pan Am: He makes the going great. God is like Coke: He's the real thing. God is like Scope: He makes you feel fresh. God is like General Electric Bulbs: He lights our paths." But one little girl said, "God is just like Hallmark Cards: He cared enough to send the very best!" That He did. He sent Christ to deliver us to heaven! We must take note of the message of heaven and the throne room in the poem on the next page.

HEAVEN

Heaven is a wonderful place,
Where the redeemed of earth shall meet.
It is a land of love and beauty,
A land of promise sweet.

In heaven we live forever,
No pain can enter in.
No crying, mourning, or sorrow,
Nor any kind of sin.

Their robes there are spotless,
The street is paved with gold,
The walls are made of jasper.
And there we'll never grow old.

No death shall ever be there,
A land of joy untold.
No tears, no darkness anywhere,
For God is the Light, I know.

There is a stream of water,
Flows out from God's throne.
We can drink it freely,
There thirst is never known.

The land called Heaven,
So rich and rare.
The richest blessing of it all,
Is that Christ and God are there.

There our joy and happiness,
Go on unendingly.
Only the ones in the Book of Life,
Heaven they will see.

(Sharon Shepherd)

Jesus Christ comforted the persecuted church in the vision of God upon His throne (4:1-11). The severe trials of the church cannot move God from his heavenly throne (4:13). One must remember that Jesus ascended to the right hand of God's throne after his resurrection (Acts 1:911; 7:55-56). John is given an opportunity to see the glory of Christ in the throne scene. He begins the real prophecy of the Revelation to give comfort to the persecuted Christians by pointing to the eternal glory of the throne of God and Christ. He assures them that God is on his throne and in control, even while Rome is their greatest enemy (4:8; Col. 1:17-18). Great trials matter little when God is in complete control.

The throne scene sets the stage for all that follows in the "drama of Redemption." Chapter one is a vision of the living, victorious Christ. The churches of Asia Minor are assured victory over the tribulations of life on earth in chapters two and three. In chapter four they are told to believe in the presence and power of God through Christ (John 14:13). They are told to believe in the redemption of Christ in chapter five. The wrath of God is visited upon the enemies of the church in chapters six through eighteen. The final and complete victory of Christ and the eternal destiny of man are given in Revelation chapters nineteen through twenty-two, regardless of their persecution (2 Chron. 32:78). Ray Summers explains that chapter four appears at this point in the Apocalypse to assure the saints of complete victory:

> Now it is time to draw the curtain and reveal the stage set for the drama. From here forward, in rapid sequence, will be presented scenes to assure the persecuted Christians that the cause of Christ is not a lost cause. Hard and bitter is to be the struggle, but when the final curtain falls at the end of the play (22:21), complete assurance of victory is demonstrated (129).

Christ revealed to John things that must shortly come to pass through an open door in heaven (4:1). The voice of Christ was distinct and intensified, inviting him to experience a higher insight of spiritual things. The figure of the "opened door" represents the opportunity of saints to serve Christ on earth and to enter heaven. It gave John the opportunity to get a glimpse of the glory and power of God (3:8; Matt. 3:16-17). In the remaining chapters, John was shown such things as the second coming of Christ, the final judgment, and the glorious church rewarded eternally.

The throne of God is "set" or placed permanently in heaven for eternity (4:23; Ps. 103:19; 119:89). The sovereignty of God is in complete control and when all is said and done on earth, the throne will still be in heaven to sustain the saved. God will be merciful and just when he judges the world and avenges the blood of the saints' persecutors.

John saw in the throne room the worship of the heavenly attendants (4:4-11). The symbol of the twenty elders is taken from the twelve patriarchs of the Old Testament. The patriarchs who were over the twelve tribes of Israel, plus the twelve apostles of the New Testament, equal the universal church in her heavenly state reigning with Christ (Matt. 19:28; Luke 22:30). The "four living creatures" are like the higher order of angels or cherubim in the visions of Isaiah and Ezekiel, which represent the worship of the saved in heaven (Isa. 6:14; Ezek. 1:5-14). Therefore, the church is praising God for the victory over her persecutors (19:15).

God is still on His throne. John wrote: "From the throne came flashes of lightning, rumblings and peals of thunder. Before the throne, seven lamps were blazing. These are the seven spirits of God" (4:5). The Spirit of God is present with us in all the power of God to deal with sin and evil in the world (4:8). His presence is illustrated by the natives in the South Pacific who were greatly disturbed when there was an eclipse of the moon. This beautiful and dependable light in the sky had suddenly and mysteriously disappeared. Naturally, it disturbed them. But those who know the nature of an eclipse understand the moon is there all the time, obscured only temporarily.

There are always shadows of doubt, sin, worldliness, tribulation, persecution, and depression that bring an eclipse to separate us from the fellowship with God. We need to remember in such times

God is present just the same, absolutely dependable and real. He is behind the eclipse of our lack of faith and obedience at all times to redeem! He never leaves us, nor forsakes us, the children of God. He lives within us through the Spirit. The blood of Christ is ever present to cleanse our life giving spirit, making us ready with a home in the throne room. Christ won our victory at the cross and the resurrection. Therefore, we are more than conquerors over the world of sin, sickness, sorrow, and death.

THE VICTORIOUS LAMB OF GOD

Christ, the Lamb of God, demonstrates the love of God who is all wise and all powerful in redeeming man from sin (5:1-14). Christians are taught to believe in this victory. Jesus Christ is the Lamb of God who comes before the throne of God and takes the book of seven seals to open it and reveal the message of redemption (John 1:12; 5:1, 67). The book is sealed securely with seven seals, which indicate security and permanency. The use of the perfect passive participle of the verb "sealed" denotes unsuccessful attempts of others to open the book (5:24). The point is that no man can know the future destiny of man until it is revealed by God, as in chapters 6-19.

The 'book' is a scroll familiar to the people of the first century. It is a type of book that Ezekiel received from God containing a message of warning, salvation, lamentations, mourning, and woe upon the rebellious and disobedient (Ezek. 2:8-3:27). It was a complete book written on both sides. It contained an extensive explanation of the redemption of man through the sacrifice of the Lamb of God.

The strong angel asked, "Who is worthy to open the book, and to loose the seals thereof?" (5:2). The only one in heaven and on earth able to open the book was Christ, the Lamb of God (5:3-5). The key to unlock the mysterious scroll was not power, but morality, righteousness, holiness, and justice, as indicated by the word "worthy." God solved the great problem of human redemption in the sacrifice of his Son (1:5; John 3:16; Rom. 3:25-26; Eph. 1:7). The situation here is almost identical to David's asking God for a revelation of God's righteousness, loving kindness, and salvation "in the roll of the book" (Ps. 40:6-12). Christ, in His preexistent state before the incarnation, responded to the challenge of the redemption of mankind. Redemption is impossible with man, angels, or demons (5:3; Matt. 19:26; Phil. 2:9-10). However, it was accomplished in the death of Jesus Christ.

There are four attributes given in this context that identify Christ as the Lamb of God (5:5-6). First, He was the Lion of Judah, which was an accepted messianic designation used in reference to the descendants of Judah, the son of Jacob, who was a "lion's whelp" (Gen. 49:8-10). This lion's whelp would lay his hand on the neck of the enemies of God's people to their defeat. Ezekiel used this same symbol in a messianic prophecy of one who would "nourish" the people of God and "devour men" who were their enemies (Ezek. 19:16; Mic. 5:8). He is strong, stately, and kingly, like a lion, and as a lion rules in the forest, Christ rules the nations of the world. Second, He is of the tribe of Judah who will rule, govern, and protect his people like a shepherd (Mic. 5:2; Matt. 2:6; Heb. 7:14). Third, He is the Root of David or a descendant of David, who would rule and give hope to the Gentiles (22:16; Isa. 11:12, 10; Matt. 1:6; Rom. 15:12). He is here identified with the mark of royalty as the Triumphant One. Fourth, He is, without controversy, the Lamb of God (5:6, 8, 12; 13:8; 14:1; John 1:29). He is seen in heaven as a sacrificed Lamb which will take away sin (Isa. 53:17; Eph. 1:7).

The message of the scroll is that Jesus Christ is victorious. He "has triumphed" to open the book and reveal the message (5:5). The verb "overcome" is the first aorist active indicative of *nikao*. The aorist tense deals with action in the past. Christ had already won the victory over all enemies of the church before the writing of the book of Revelation. He won the victory in his sacrifice on the cross (Col. 2:14-15). He conquered Satan who is the source of all enemies to Christianity at the cross. The death of Christ on the cross is the center of the message in the book of Revelation (5:9-10). Mathias Rissi explains the word *nikan,* as used in this book, to describe Christ's death on the cross in the following:

It is in his death that Christ overcomes his enemies, the worldnot on a bloody eschatological battlefield, not through condemnation and annihilation, but through redemption. The word "nikan", therefore, never designates any destructive judgment upon the enemies. John has consistently maintained this view throughout the whole book. For him there is only one victory of Christ; it was won in the past and resulted in the debilitation of all enemy powers, once and for all (8).

This is the heart of the message of Revelation. Christ has the power ("seven horns"), perfect vision ("seven eyes"), and knowledge of God ("seven Spirits") to rule the earth since his crucifixion (5:6). Christ is worthy to take the scroll from the hand of God and reveal the message (5:5-7). The saints can now learn the victorious outcome of their present fiery trial. The final victory of redemption from sin and destruction of their enemies is now being revealed to them from heaven. In the next chapter, I intend to disclose the saints' victory over their enemies as they stand in the presence of God. It is awesome that we, who can kneel before the presence of God, can stand up to anything. Why be fearful?

⚜ *Chapter 5* ⚜

Victory In The Church

The book of Revelation shows Jesus Christ among the churches (1:13, 20). It is an encouragement to the believers in a hostile world and a warning to the careless and negligent Believers who are tempted to fall away into an easy conformity to the world. It reveals that the control and destiny of the nations, among which the church existed, is in God's hand. There are two important questions answered in the book concerning Christ and his church: 1) Where is her Lord? 2) What is going to become of the church? It is my task in this section to show that God rules over all and will deliver his church through Jesus Christ.

The greatest number of references of the verb *nikao* is in chapters two through four in the message given to the seven churches of Asia Minor (2:7, 11, 17, 26; 3:5, 12, 21; 21:7). These congregations were told by Christ that they could be victorious, despite their problems and the circumstances of the world. The verb is applied to Christ and the believers in a martyrological sense in reference to overcoming all enemies even in death (12:11; 13:7). Christ expected the churches to correct their problems and win the victory. He gave them an optimistic message that he is with them to help them overcome. "Remember, optimism is an intellectual choice" (Diana Schneider). Christ gave these believers the opportunity to make this intelligent choice. They must choose freedom!

The verb *nikao* is an intransitive verb meaning to be a victor, to prevail or conquer in two ways. First, the Believer can conquer in a battle or contest, looking to Christ. Second, the Believer can win in a legal action, which is winning when accused (Rom. 3:4). It is also an intransitive verb denoting the effect victory has on the Believer in two ways. First, the Believer overcomes the world in which he lives, actively winning over the sum total of everything opposed to God, especially Satan (11; 13:7; 17:14; Luke 11:22; 1 John 4:4; 5:4). Second, in the passive sense, it means to be conquered or beaten. It is used only once in the New Testament (Rom. 12:21). In this text evil has been overcome. Beloved, Jesus died to overcome the world (John 16:33).

John used the verb "overcome" by metonymy, meaning a personal victorious principle. That is, Christ is the means for winning a victory (but compare also the custom of speaking of the emperor's *nike* as the power that grants him the victory) in every aspect of the Believers lives (Bauer 541). Believers are the ones who overcome in the context of the Revelation (2:11; 2:26; 3:5; 3:12, 21; 5:5; 6:2; 21:7). Believers cannot afford to become weary in well doing or to be unfaithful to Christ. Victory is lost outside of Christ! Faith is the victory to those who are obedient to God and His lamb.

CHRIST WITH THE CHURCH

Believers in Christ were the recipients of the Revelation (1:4, 11-20). The number "seven" is a symbol for completeness, which indicates that all the churches of Asia Minor were recipients of the book and represented the church as a whole. Ray Summers describes the boundary of these seven churches which are situated on the most populous, wealthy, and influential part of the west central region of the province. "They were the best points on the circuit to serve as centers of communication with seven districts: Pergamum for the north, Thyatira for an inland district on the northeast and east, Sardis for the wide middle valley of the Hermus, Philadelphia for upper Lydia, Laoddicea for the Lycus Valley, Ephesus for the lower Maeander valleys and coasts, and Smyrna for the North Ionian coasts" (Summers 86). The assembly of Believers in all ages benefit from this message.

Christ speaks a blessing to "the one who reads aloud" the words of the Revelation (1:3 ESV). There is something to be said for the reading "aloud" this message. Reading the message of God aloud was common in the first century, especially in the assembly of these suffering saints. Perhaps, this exercise contained a healing for their painful hearts. The Believer stands in awe of God, in the presence of his peers, and reads this victory message aloud for comfort and healing. Thus, the saints acknowledge God in relieving their doubts, anxiety, and fears.

The "kingdom" existed "in Jesus" at the time of this writing (1:9). That the church was successful in overcoming persecution, through the means provided by Jesus Christ to meet tribulation, is evident in John's use of the preposition "in." The preposition describes the intimate relationship the church has with God and Christ. It conveys the idea that Christ has the power to equip and furnish the needs of the saints in persecution. The church is in his presence. John and his fellow Christians were preserved in the kingdom of Christ, redeemed by his blood, and made a kingdom (1:5-6). He freed the Believers from sin. Sin no longer rules over the saints. There is no more pain, distress, or guilt from sin experienced in their hearts. He rules, or is in charge of earthly kings, in order to grant victory over any hardship and persecution caused by these kings. He is with Believers, as he promised to help them overcome persecution. Praise God, free indeed!

Christ was in the "midst of the candlesticks" as Ruler, Chief, or Prince of peace, comfort, and victory, having defeated the kings of the earth (1:11-13; 2:1, 5; 11:4). The symbol of the "candlesticks" is identified as the church (1:20). The word "midst" (*meso*) is the dative singular neuter case of the adjective *mesos*. It means that Christ is the One in the middle, among, or at the center of the church as he was on the center of the throne among the four living creatures (5:6; 7:17). *Mesos* used in the genitive denotes the close personal relationship Christ has with the church as Mediator (1 Tim. 2:5), one who interposes to reconcile two adverse parties. Christ is the medium of communication between the church and her enemies (Gal. 3:19-20; Heb. 8:6). He is her consolation, the redeemer of her enemies, therefore, a mediator to bring both to God in heaven based on their obedience to his will.

Christ, the Son of Man, was seen among the "seven golden candlesticks" (*lunchnia*), which means light. It is used two ways in Revelation: first, symbolically of the church which bears the light of Christ in a dark world of sin (18:23-24; 22:5; Matt. 5:14-16; Mark 4:21-29; Luke. 8:16); and second, metaphorically of Jesus Christ, the source of light or guidance given to the church (21:23; 5:6; 7:17; 14:4) and the world (John 8:12). Believers reflect this light with the help of Christ as the moon reflects light with the help of the sun. Christ will guide the church to victory over persecution.

The seven golden lamp stands have a relationship to the seven branched lamp stands in the tabernacle (Exod. 25:31ff) and Zechariah's vision (ch. 4) of the two witnesses (11:4). That Old Testament model has now become symbolic of the freedom and complete light which the church has in Christ. The seven churches of Asia appear in Revelation as seven lamp stands directed and visited by Christ in judgment ((2:1). He threatened to remove their lamp stand or remove them from the circle of the churches if they were not faithful to God (2:5). Christ is seen walking in the midst of the churches with clear vision of the life and works of each congregation.

Christ is seen holding the "seven stars" and the "seven golden candlesticks" in his right hand to direct, support, protect, and strengthen them (1:20). The "seven stars" represent the messengers (angels) who in turn represent the ministers or elders of the congregations. John again uses an Old Testament symbol to represent the wise leadership of the church under the direction of Christ (Dan. 12:3). Joseph Henry

Thayer gives the significance of the lamp and the stars in reference to Christ in an Old Testament perspective:

> To a "lamp" are likened the eye, i.e. which shows the body which way to move and turn, Mt. 6:22; Lk. 11:34; the prophecies of the O.T., inasmuch as they afforded at least some knowledge relative to the glorious return of Jesus from heaven down even to the time when by the Holy Spirit that same light, like the day and the daystar, shone upon the hearts of men, the light by which the prophets themselves had been enlightened and which was necessary to the full perception of the true meaning of their prophecies, 2 Pet.1:19; to the brightness of a lamp that cheers the beholders a teacher is compared, whom even those rejoiced in who were unwilling to comply with his demands, Jn. 5:35; Christ, who will hereafter illumine his followers, the citizens of the heavenly kingdom, with his own glory, Rev. 21:23 (384).

It is important to notice that the lamp stands are described as "golden" (1:12). This is another reference to the precious metal used in the Old Testament tabernacle (Ex. 25). The gold in this text represents the precious nature and tremendous value of the churches. The metal is used in several passages describing the victory of the church in heaven as she receives such things as a golden crown and a dwelling place with streets of gold (3:18; 17:4; 18:12, 16; 21:18, 21). The basic message is that the church is precious to Christ, and he will protect her with divine guidance.

ESTABLISHMENT OF THE CHURCH

One cannot separate Christ and His church which was established during the time of the Roman Empire. The church exists to exalt and proclaim Christ as Lord in the entire world. John was a member of the "kingdom" or church at the time of this writing (1:9). Jesus placed those whom he loosed from their sins in the kingdom (1:56). He purchased people from every tribe, tongue, and nation to reign with him in the kingdom (5:9-10). They are seen reigning with Christ in heaven, having overcome the persecution of the Roman world (20:6). Christ is present in every assembly of the saints to grant peace and victory. Praise and worship is a victorious celebration every first day of the week.

The kingdom, or the reign and sovereignty of God in the church, is divine, eternal, and unconquerable. It is the kingdom that Daniel compares to the kingdoms of the world which are human in origin and temporary. Each of these kingdoms was overcome and incorporated by each succeeding kingdom (Dan. 2:31-44). It was in the days of these Roman Kings that Christ established his everlasting Kingdom (Matt. 16:18-19; Mark 1:14-15; Luke. 13:1f). Edward J. Young is a good representation of the scholarship that interprets Daniel's prophecy of the kingdoms which preceded the establishment of the church (2:44) in the days of the Roman Empire: "The head of gold is the neoBabylonian Empire. The breast and arms is the MedoPersian Empire. The belly and thighs is the Grecian Empire. The legs and feet is the Roman Empire" (Young 76). The cross of Christ is powerful to break through the powers of the day from head to toe. The Lamb died for the assembly of the saints, giving them the rule, reign, and character of God. He exalts them now and forever in eternity.

Daniel prophesied that Christ's kingdom would ultimately break in pieces and destroy the Roman Empire (Dan. 2:44f). After suffering greatly the kingdom of Christ will defeat Rome and live in heaven eternally (1:9). The kingdom of God is of Divine origin and eternal in nature and duration. The kingdom is divine, therefore, it is eternal. It will, furthermore, not be conquered by others but will ever be in the hands of the same people, the true Israel of God, the Church. On the other hand, it will break in pieces and destroy other kingdoms, especially those of this world.

The church was severely persecuted under the Roman rule because she would not worship the gods of Rome, such as Roma. John and many other Christians shared the tribulation which was inflicted upon them by Satan using the Roman Emperors (1:9; 12:13, 17; 13:7). Antipas, a faithful witness of Christ, was killed in Pergamum where Satan dwelled because he confessed Jesus Christ as Lord which was in opposition to Domitian, the lord of the Romans (2:13; 17:14). Persecution was real to the seven churches of Asia. Jesus Christ gave the victory to the church that was very much despised by the Jews and the Romans. To the Romans, Christianity was "a sort of atheism because it acknowledged no visible gods. To the Jews, who traditionally worshipped a single invisible God, Christianity was clearly a perversion of the religion of the patriarchs and prophets" (Kerr 17).

The condition of the first recipients of the Revelation, early Christians, in Asia Minor (1:4) was very critical. The Roman Government tolerated Christianity for several years as a part of the Jewish religion, which was a legalized religion in the Roman Empire. However, when the Romans discovered that Christianity was not a revised copy of Judaism, the Christians became hated by the government. Ray Summers reviews ten reasons for the antagonism directed toward the Christians:

> Christianity was an illegal religion. Its efforts to proselyte others into its ranks was contrary to Roman law. Christianity aspired to universality. Christians taught that the kingdom of Christ was the main thing throughout the whole earth, not just as an aid to the Roman State. Christianity was an exclusive religion. Christians refused to mingle freely with heathen social life and customs. They were accused of all manner of evil things such as cannibalism, sexual orgies, human sacrifice, atheism, and treason. Christians refused to serve in the Roman armies. Christians were recruited chiefly from the poor and outcast being looked down upon by those who regarded themselves as the respectable. Christians refused to compromise with the Roman armies. Christians were recruited chiefly

from the poor and outcast being looked down upon by those who regarded themselves as worse than the Jews. Christians were regarded as wild fanatics because of their enthusiasm to shock the sensibilities of the passive philosophers of the day. Christians interfered with the temporal interests of many of the Roman priests, makers and sellers of idolatrous artifacts and sacrificial animals. Christians refused to worship the emperor (87-88).

Christianity did not die as hoped for by the Romans. The church grew in the empire to the amazement of both the Jews and Romans. The saints demonstrated a triumphant faith during the Roman persecution. They preached and practiced the doctrine of Christ in purity in everyday life. In support of this victory Edward Gibbon gives five excellent reasons for the tremendous growth of Christianity in the Roman Empire:

Christians inherited an inflexible zeal for God which they inherited from the Jews. They felt an arduous duty to preserve themselves pure and undefiled from the practice of idolatry. Christians believed and taught the doctrine of a future life which opposed the ignorance, the errors, and the uncertainty of the ancient philosophers. This armed the disciples against the fear of death knowing that hope of heaven would relieve their suffering. The primitive church had the ability to exercise miraculous gifts and preach with divine inspiration. The austere morals of the first Christians were a demonstration of their faith by their virtues which purified the heart and directed the actions of the believer. The primitive Christians were dead to the business and pleasures of the world; but their love of action, which could never be entirely extinguished, soon revived, and found a new occupation in the government of the church (143-91).

A MESSAGE OF VICTORY

The theme of the letters to the seven churches of Asia is the power Christ gave them to overcome the world. The verb "overcome" is used at the end of each letter to express Christ's expectation that they will have the victory. This present tense participle indicates a continuous or repeated action in the present time. Therefore, the overcoming process was taking place at the time John was writing these letters and will continue until eternity. The point in this thesis is that the church is in the process of overcoming at the present time. What must they overcome? What blessing did Christ promise the triumphant? These two theme questions will be answered in this section. The believers addressed in this book are truly victorious! Jesus assures His followers of The Blessings of the Overcomer:

1. They shall "eat of the tree of life in the paradise of God" (2:7).

2. They shall not be hurt by the "second death" (2:11).

3. They shall be given the "hidden manna" (2:17).

4. They will be given "authority over the nations" (2:26).

5. They shall be "dressed in white garments" (3:5).

6. They shall be "pillars in the temple of God" (3:12).

7. They shall "sit down with Jesus on the throne" (3:21).

In each of these letters, the Christian is pictured as the one who is victorious (2:7, 11, 17, 26; 3:5, 12, 21). Christ is the means for their winning a victory (2:1). Believers have power through the blood of

Christ to conquer the world, Satan, and the beast, or rulers of Rome (15:2). Henry Thayer gives such a definition of *nikao*:

> Absolutely to carry off the victory, come off victorious: of Christ, victorious over all his foes, Rev. 3:21; 6:2; and hath so conquered that he now has the right and power to open etc. Rev. 5:5; of Christians, that hold fast their faith even unto death against the power of their foes, and their temptations and persecutions, Rev. 2:7, 11, 17, 26; 3:5, 12, 21; 21:7; to conquer and thereby free themselves from the power of the beast, Rev. 15:2; when one is arraigned or goes to law, to win the case, maintain one's cause, Rom. 3:4 (425-26).

The first letter of the Revelation is addressed to the church at **Ephesus** which is described as a congregation zealous for orthodoxy without love. Ephesus, the first and greatest metropolis of Asia Minor, was the capital of the Roman Province of Asia. Since it was on the main trade route and possessed the best harbor of Asia, it was very wealthy and was known as "The Market of Asia." It was a self governing city and was known for its gross immorality and wickedness.

The Roman Empire promoted the worship of many Greek gods of immorality. The city of Ephesus was the center for the worship of the goddess Diana, or Artemis. The city contained a large Greek built stadium (425' by 225' with 120 columns) for the worship of the goddess (Acts 19). Demetrius caused a persecution to be brought against Paul because he preached against their idolatry and superstition (19:24-25).

The heart of Christ's message to Ephesus was for them to overcome their present situation. The message can be summarized under two main themes: areas they had already overcome and things which they needed to overcome in order to be rewarded. They had many positive achievements in the areas they had overcome (2:23). They had toiled and labored very hard in the cause of Christ under difficult times and had faced much opposition. The church at Ephesus, under the oversight of elders, was busy preaching sound doctrine and spreading the gospel in the community (Acts 18-20). These Christians exercised patience in bearing up under the hardships for Christ. The word "patience" denotes the ability to remain faithful under great difficulties or heavy burdens. They were also strong to stand against heresy. They could not support false apostles (2:2). It says much for this church that they were alert enough to test these teachers of false doctrine and reject such teaching.

The work of the Nicolaitans was hated at Ephesus (2:6). This church was commended by Christ in contending for the faith against such heresy. Donald Guthrie parallels the Nicolaitans with the heresies of Balaam in the Old Testament. He says the Ephesians:

> ... hate the Nicolaitans, who are linked in 2:15 with those who hold the teaching of Balaam. It may be significant that the Greek root behind `Nicolaus' and the Hebrew root behind `Balaam' possibly both mean `to conquer the people'. Certainly Balaam, according to Numbers 25:15, seduced the people and caused them to sin. According to the message to Pergamum the false teaching was connected with meat offered to idols and with immorality. It was clearly a threat to the Christian faith. At a time when the church was in its infancy it was of utmost importance that true worship and true morals should be jealously guarded, and both were under attack (73).

The church at Ephesus is a good example to any permissive society to continue to stand for the moral purity and doctrine of Christ under great opposition. The Ephesians overcame the teaching of Balaam rather than Balaam overcoming the people. The church grew, even in the Roman Empire, because these Christians took a firm stand to preserve purity of doctrine and of practice in their daily lives.

Yet, there is another theme to the message of victory given to Ephesus. The saints at Ephesus had lost their first love (2:4). There are two possible interpretations to be kept in mind concerning this passage. They had either lost their first love for Christ, or they had lost their first love for one another. Perhaps, John has both in mind. The Bible clearly teaches that one cannot love Christ and hate his brother (1 John 4:20-21); orthodoxy without love is worthless. The letter points out that the Ephesians must overcome this attitude in order to have eternal victory in heaven.

Christ gave three directions for the Ephesians to correct their spiritual condition (2:5). First, they were told to remember their fallen condition. Christ wanted them to remember the heights from which they had fallen from the grace of God. They were in a spiritual and moral decline because they had fallen from their love for God and one another. Memory is a great asset to repentance. The wayward Jewish nation remembered the brighter days in a better land back home and wept by the willows (Ps. 137). The Jews finally returned to God. The Ephesians were in a position to be ruined completely if they did not remember, repent, and return to God. Second, they were told to repent. Repentance brought the actual change of will and action to their lives. The word repent implies that they must want to change their spiritual condition. Third, they were told to return to their first works which were prompted by their first love (Eph. 1:15-16). Christ wanted them to continue to obey the will, or law, of God (14:12). The truth of God must be practiced in Christian virtues (22:11). Jesus warned them that this condition would remain unless they repented.

Jesus Christ promised the victor that he would "eat of the tree of life in the Paradise of God" as an incentive to return to God (2:7). This was a promise only to those who would overcome all foes and world conflicts in faithfulness to God. The "tree of life" was the life giving tree which thrived in Eden (22:1-3; Gen. 2:9; 3:22-24; Luke 16:22). While it was forfeited by an act of disobedience, now it can be regained by an act of obedience. Since Jesus promised the victor spiritual food to sustain him in heaven, it was worthy of their time to be loyal to Christ on earth.

The second letter is addressed to the church in **Smyrna** which was known for spiritual wealth in the midst of much poverty and affliction (2:8-11). The city of Smyrna, known as "The Ornament of Asia," was one of the most beautiful cities of the province founded by Alexander the Great. It was an inland seaport and a great trading center about 40 miles north of Ephesus. Its feet were at the sea, its body lay in the Hermus valley, and its head was upon Mt. Pagos, which was crowned with all the pagan temples and noble buildings. Pagan religion flourished in the city since it was the home of the temple of Roma and other gods which guarded various activities of the Roman citizens.

The city of Smyrna was known as a "free city" because of it faithfulness and loyalty to Rome. Smyrna, which was the birth place of Homer, had a large Jewish community known for its municipal pride and vanity. Unlike Ephesus, which disappeared completely, Smyrna is still a prosperous city now called Izmir, Turkey. Smyrna was the home of Polycarp, its aged bishop, who served as an elder of the church for some forty or fifty years. He was killed for his faith on February 22, 156 AD, at the age of 86. History describes Polycarp's loyalty to Christ, as he faced burning at the stake, in a statement written by the church at Smyrna:

> It tells of the arrest of Polycarp and how, because of his age, the officers tried to persuade him to say "Lord Caesar," and to sacrifice to the gods that he might be spared. He refused to do so and when brought before the Proconsul his freedom was offered if he would revile Christ. To this Polycarp said, "For eighty and six years have I been his servant, and he has done me no wrong, and how can I blaspheme my King who saved me?" With this he was bound and burned (Mattox 65).

The outstanding characteristic of this church was that it was not condemned by the Lord. What a tribute! They had overcome Satan (2:9). The Lord admonished them to continue in the faith to receive a crown of life in the end (2:10). The "ten days" indicate a short period of time, which showed that Christ was in control instead of the persecutors. They had nothing to fear because the resurrected Lord was their strength (2:8; 1:17-18; 2:1).

The real victory of the church at Smyrna was not only their ability to overcome Satan but also to overcome poverty. Poverty in such a wealthy city was their first form of tribulation (2:9). They were probably from the lower class that had their goods despoiled by their persecutors, a common practice in the Roman Empire (Heb. 10:32ff.). However, these believers had faith in spiritual victory over the materialism of the world:

> It is often more difficult to reach the poorer people with the gospel than the more affluent middle classes. The main lesson in the message to this church is that there is no correlation between material prosperity and spiritual riches, for the Lord pronounces these poverty stricken believers to be rich. This assertion of their spiritual superiority is borne out by the absence of any command to repent, a feature shared only by the church at Philadelphia (Guthrie 75).

The second form of the tribulation brought upon the Smyrneans was the blasphemy or insult and slander of those who claimed to be Jews, but were nothing more than "a synagogue of Satan" (2:9). These persecutors were Jews outwardly like those condemned by Paul (Rom. 2:25-29). They denied the real membership of the Jewish race by allowing Satan, the accuser of Christians (12:10), to have the advantage in their worship assembly. Christians who refused to worship the emperor in such assemblies were regarded as atheists and many suffered death. They may have suffered imprisonment and death in this life but, if faithful, they will be crowned with victory in heaven (2:10). Christ delivered them from the second death which is the lake burning with fire and brimstone (2:11; 21:8). Smyrna was the rich, poor church that Christ crowned with victory.

Pergamum was the church that remained true to the name of Christ (2:12-17). These victors were faithful to the name of Christ while living at the foot of Satan's throne (2:13). Historically, Pergamum, the greatest city in all the district of Asia, was the center of Caesar worship. Satan's throne or power was used in seducing unstable souls into pagan worship with its immoral rites. Pergamum had been the provincial capital for 400 years and was the home of the great temple to Athene, the altar of Zeus, and the worship center for Asclepius, the god of healing, who used the serpent as his emblem. Satan, the power behind Rome's persecution of the church, is also identified with the serpent that deceived the whole world (12:9). The city survived and exists today under the name of Bergamo as a very small, poor Turkish city.

Christ commends the church at Pergamum for overcoming Satan's throne (2:13a). The word "throne" denotes the seat of authority or power of Satan. This city of Satan, who moves in the world to oppose the church, was rampant with idolatry and all its attendant evils (Job 1:6-7; Matt. 4:8; 1 Pet. 5:8). The city was dominated by the temple of Zeus, the savior god, with a 40foot altar carved like a throne into the mountain facing the area.

The victory over the idolatry promoted by Satan is seen in the Christians who did not deny the name of Christ (2:13b). They were unlike Israel who denied God's holy name by blending in with the world around them (Ezek. 36:16-21). The Christians of Pergamum were better than the pagans around them because they did not dishonor the name of Christ. They openly proclaimed the Lordship of Christ in opposition to the emperor's request to be their lord. In this way the Christians assured the world that the ultimate sovereignty rested with Christ, not Rome.

The second commendation of Christ was the faithfulness of the Christians at Pergamum (2:13c). Antipas was an example of a faithful witness of Christ even as he faced death. He did not renounce his loyalty and confessed Christ before the emperors. The church was encouraged by the example of Antipas not to allow persecution to turn her aside after Satan. The opposition to Christianity did not lead to any slackening of zeal or renouncing of their faith or trust in Christ, the exalted Lord.

Jesus Christ, however, had some things against the church at Pergamum such as the false doctrines of Balaam and the doctrine of the Nicolaitans (2:14-15). Balaam caused the Israelites to compromise their faith for personal gain. The Midianites made sacrifice to their gods and persuaded the Israelites to join them in the immoral ceremonies of their pagan worship. The Balaamites taught at Pergamum that it was acceptable to participate in pagan worship services. This compromise of spiritual doctrine and morality was to be stopped at once (2:16). Christ wanted them to be different from the Balaamites who were willing to make material gain at the cost of spirituality. Believers are victorious only when they stand firm for the doctrine and spirituality of Christ. The world awaits the doctrine of Christ dressed in rich spirituality.

The doctrine of the Nicolaitans came from Nicolas, a Jewish convert from Antioch who taught that the gospel lifts man above the moral law, giving him a license to worship idols and to commit the vilest of moral sins (Acts 6:5). They put no restrictions between Christ and fellowship with pagan festivals of idolatry and sexual immorality. The Nicolaitans argued that restrictions in the Christian lifestyle, or code of behavior, would make them unpopular with the Romans. They robbed the church of its moral and ethical standards commanded by Christ. The Christians at Pergamum must repent of teaching these doctrines or be removed as a faithful church (2:16). Their safety and victory were in Christ. The promise to the victors at Pergamum was threefold (2:17). First, the faithful were promised "the hidden manna," which was a symbol taken from the life of the children of Israel to suggest the satisfaction of every spiritual need (Exod. 16:11-15). In other words, the Lord will provide for the needs of his faithful ones, as he did for Israel in the wilderness, and will sustain them unto eternal life in heaven (John 6:31-35). Second, the faithful were promised "a white stone," which was a token of victory and freedom in divine honor and favor. It was given to the warrior who returned from the battle with victory over the enemy. The Christians at Pergamum could easily interpret this symbol because they mined white stone and used it as a commercial product. It was also used to designate the winner of a race or contest. Third, a "new name" was promised to the victor. Names and character change when men advance spiritually. For example, Abram's name was changed to Abraham, and Jacob's was changed to Israel (Gen. 17:5; 32:28). God gave these men a new name as they advanced in character. This new name represented a new character given to the people of God in secret between them and God. Believers have the character of God as winners.

The fourth letter, one of the longest, was written to the church at **Thyatira**. Thyatira, the least important city in the business world of the time, is still a flourishing city in Turkey. It was known for manufacturing shops and skilled workmen. Woolen goods and the famous purple dye were the chief products of the city. It was the home of Lydia, a seller of purple (Acts 16:14). Spiritually, the city was known for communal meals which were usually held in temples of idols. Sacrifices were offered to the gods, and the sacrificial meat was eaten (1 Cor. 8). These meals often degenerated into drunken orgies.

Christ came to inspect this congregation as one with penetrating vision, strong and durable feet, and one who searches the reins and heart (2:18, 23; 1:14-15). Christ knew the work and faithfulness of the church from the inside of man (2:19). The Christian qualities that existed among the church at Thyatira were praiseworthy. He praised them for their love, which is the garment of exceptional beauty, the very essence of Christianity (1 John 4:20-21; 53). A true love for both God and man is a basic foundation for Christianity (Mark 12:30-31). The saints had an abiding faith in Christ. The word "faith" denotes the trust and confidence they had in God and implies that which causes trust and faithfulness, reliability, commitment, and love for God (Gal. 5:6). There was also a segment of the church faithful in the ministering to the needs of others as we find in other New Testament examples (Heb. 6:19; 1 Pet. 4:9-11). Christ praised them for their patience. The word "patience" is the foundation of all Christian virtues held by early Believers. "Patience is steadfastness, constancy, and endurance. In the New Testament, these are the characteristics of a man who is unswerved from his deliberate purpose and his loyalty to faith and piety by even the greatest trials and sufferings (Rev. 2:2, 19; 13:10; 14:12)" (Thayer 644).

The letter to Thyatira explains what it means to overcome by keeping the words of Christ faithfully unto the end which they had done, except in one area (2:25). They needed to repent of their tolerating the teaching of Jezebel (2:20-24). The self-styled prophetess among them probably was not Jezebel. John used this symbolic name in allusion to Ahab's wife (1 Kings 16:30-33) who introduced Israel to Baal worship. In Thyatira she was corrupting the church by teaching the saints to commit fornication and to eat meat sacrificed to idols. They were not guilty of her sin; they only tolerated her erroneous teaching. The challenge of the church in any age is to overcome false teaching and the world without fellowship in the sin. The church must not lack the courage and zeal to carry out congregational discipline.

Christ makes two promises to those who overcome at Thyatira (2:27-28). The victor is promised the authority to rule the nations, which is a symbolic way of saying that the faithful Christians will share in Christ's victory to rule over the world forces that were opposed to God. These Christians were vindicated before their persecutors as they preached the Gospel against the spiritual "world rulers" who were directed by Satan (Eph. 6:10-18). They would share in Christ's power to crush to pieces all persecuting heathen nations (Ps. 2:8-9). Christ would also give the faithful "the morning star," another token of triumph. Christ himself is the morning star (22:16). There are two possible meanings to this symbol: they would be like Christ (1 John 3:2), or Christ would guide them through the hour of trials. The latter is probably intended, meaning they would recognize that Christ should be followed rather than the false leadership of the Roman Empire.

The assembly of the saints at **Sardis** was dead, and the Lord had no commendation for them (3:16). Sardis was situated some 1500 feet above sea level on Mt. Tmolus in the Hermus Valley, which made it easily defended and virtually impregnable. It was a wealthy but spiritually degenerate city. By the time of John's writing, the church had absorbed the city's unhealthy atmosphere and had died spiritually. Sardis was the ancient capital of the kingdom of Lydia and the seat of the legendary King Croesus who was known for his great wealth. Croesus had retreated to his wealthy fortress in total confidence that all was safe when he was invaded by Cyrus in 546 BC. Cyrus had discovered a narrow crevice in the rock, and by night his men ascended the mountain through it. There were no watchmen to give warning, and the city fell in one night. The fall of Sardis was due to overconfidence (3:2). Their strength became their weakness, and the enemy came as a thief in the night and overcame them. The letter to the church is rooted in the history and character of the city.

The challenge presented to this church was to wake up and strengthen what was left of their imperfect works (3:2). The word "perfected" means to carry out to fullness and completeness. They may have started many good works but had completed nothing. They were simply "playing church" in form without doing the work God has planned for the church. They must overcome their lost mission for God.

Christ admonishes the spiritually dead by promising to reward victory to the faithful few (3:4-5). It is a truth of God that in a dead, wicked, and indifferent congregation there are a few members who, in humility and obscurity, still try to do the will of God. It is possible for these few people to strengthen that which remains alive and be saved within a dead church. There is always a possibility that the faithful few can bring the dead to life once again by their great works of faithfulness. This is the group that will overcome for the Lord. Christ promised those who overcome that they would be dressed in white, which denotes spiritual purity, cleanliness, and joy (3:5). The symbolic meaning of the white garments is best explained in the context of the book of Revelation which John uses in five other passages: (1) The purity of the white garments is used in contrast to

94

the shame of worldliness (3:18). (2) The white garments are a reward in heaven, a place of purity (4:4). (3) A white robe is given to each of the martyred souls for their faithfulness to the word and testimony of God (6:11). (4) The white robes are washed in the cleansing blood of Christ (7:9, 13-14). (5) The victorious Christians celebrated in heaven being "clothed in fine linen, white and pure" (19:8, 14). Therefore, John is describing the spiritual purity of the faithful at Sardis.

Some saints at Sardis were worthy of the white garments because of their faithfulness (3:4). They had not participated in the pagan worship and worldliness of the day and they were not indifferent. Because they were true to God, the faithful Sardis Believer would have a permanent walk with Christ and the heavenly host (7:14; 19:7-8). They could easily understand these symbols because of the white toga worn by the Romans at festival times and when the Persian kings allowed their favored companions to walk with them in the royal gardens. The faithful were also promised that Christ would confess them before the Father (3:5). It is a great honor to be recorded in the book of life which is the remembrance of the great infinite mind of God (Exod. 32:32; Mal. 3:16-17; Luke 10:20; Phil. 4:3). The names found written in the book of life in the end will be saved (20:15; 21:27). Believers may be added to the list of martyrs for refusing Emperor Worship, but Christ will confess them to God.

The church at **Philadelphia** was the church with an open door for the spreading of the Gospel (3:7-13). Philadelphia, by definition of its name, was the city of brotherly love. It was a walled city of the district of Lydia, situated on the Cogamus River. It was founded about 140 BC by Attalus Philadelphos. The city was located in a rich farming district and was known for its vineyards. It was destroyed by a great earthquake in AD 17, and for many years following, the area was plagued with earth tremors that forced repeated evacuations. The city received new names twice to honor the emperors Neocaesarea and Flavia. Philadelphia survives today as the modern city in Turkey called Allah Shehr.

Jesus Christ is identified to the church at Philadelphia as "he that is holy" (3:7). The word "holy" means different and separated from the world, especially the Roman kings (17:14; Isa. 6:3). Holiness is an attribute of the deity of Christ who is also the One "that is true" (6:10). The word "true" means that he is genuine as opposed to that which is shadowy or fake. Christ is in the position of authority by holding "the key of David" which was given to him by the Father (Matt. 28:18). He alone has the power to open doors of opportunity to the church and to admit men into heaven or to deny them entrance. That the government of the church was upon Christ, not Rome (Isa. 9:6; Acts 2:47; Eph. 1:22-23), would be a source of assurance, encouragement, and victory to a suffering church.

The church at Philadelphia is like Smyrna in that the Lord commended her without any condemnation. Christ presented her with an open door because she had little power, had kept his word, and did not deny his name (3:8). The Philadelphians had a great opportunity for the gospel because they had little physical, material, or worldly strength, but great spiritual strength. It took a lot of moral and spiritual courage and loyalty to God not to deny Christ in a world forcing its citizens to bow to its leaders as deity. Their moral sovereignty was God. In these matters they had already experienced victory in Christ.

Christ gave the saints who overcome at Philadelphia some great promises of victory (3:9-12). He promised to be with them and help them to triumph over foes (3:9). They were like those in Smyrna who were subjected to the slanderous lies of the Jews who had become bitter enemies of Christianity. Christ assures them in common Jewish thought that the tables would be reversed and that the proud Jews would bow to him (Isa. 60:14; Phil. 2:9-11). Those who accept Christ, both Jew and Gentile, are the true people of God (Rom. 2:28-29).

Christ promised to visit this church quickly (3:11). He exhorted them to hold fast to the profession of their faith and hold on to their crown. It is evident that Christ considered the church at Philadelphia to be faithful from the fact that he told them to guard their crown. It was not a matter of someone's stealing their crown, but of God's taking it away because of unfaithfulness. The coming of Christ is cited for at least two reasons: it is a warning to sinners within and without the church (Matt. 24:48-51), and it is a comfort to the oppressed to encourage them to be faithful (Jas. 5:8). In this text it serves to be more of a comfort because of their present circumstances of persecution.

To those who were in the process of overcoming, Christ promised to exalt them to be a pillar in the temple of God (3:12a). This is a promise to be incorporated into a permanent position in the eternal kingdom. The word "pillar," a column or permanent structure, was used to describe persons of authority and influence who supported the true church. This was a great honor bestowed on Christians by the Lord (3:12; 10:1; Gal. 2:9; 1 Tim. 3:15). They were instructed to support the church in that time which would give them the security of a permanent dwelling in heaven. The victorious church will be exalted to a position in heaven from which no friend will depart and into which no enemy will enter.

The victorious Christians will be given a name of distinction and identity as God's children (3:12b). The "name of God" identifies them as Christians or children of God (2:17; 7:34; 14:1; 22:4; Gal. 3:26-27). The name known only to Christ identifies his followers as his own possession and as citizens in the "city of God, the new Jerusalem" (19:12). This is a glorification of Christ's church (Heb. 12:22-23). It is definitely worthwhile to continue to keep the words of Christ's message to this church for it is a message of victory (3:13).

The assembly of believers at **Laodicea** had a closed heart, an outgrowth of the exceeding riches of the membership (3:14-22). The church was established in a prominent city of commerce, which was the financial center of the Roman province of Asia and was one of the wealthiest cities of the time. The city was founded by Antiochus II of Syria in 250 BC. He named it after his wife Laodicea, who later poisoned him. It was located on the Lycus River. The wealthy Laodiceans refused help from Rome when they were destroyed by an earthquake in AD 61, preferring to pay their own way. Laodicea was also known for the manufacturing of clothing, especially its tunics called trimata, and for its sheep with their black glossy wool. The city contained a great medical school known for famous ointments for the eyes and ears. These characteristics of the city are reflected in Christ's message to the church.

There is no direct information on the founding of the church in Laodicea. It was probably founded during Paul's stay in Ephesus (Acts 19:8-10). She was a sister congregation to Colossae (Col. 4:16). Because the church had absorbed the culture and attributes of the city, she had the sad distinction of being the only church of which Christ had nothing good to say. In fact, it made him sick enough to vomit (3:16). Christ, the true and faithful witness, had firsthand knowledge of her fallen condition and had to report this information to warn other churches (3:14-15a). Christ is aware of our active faith and awards victory.

Christ, exposing the true character of the church, said she was neither hot nor cold (3:15-16). The readers of the letter could easily understand this figure because of the hot springs of Hierapolis which had a terminus in Laodicea. The springs absorbed lime and became moderately warm. The natural reaction to this lukewarm water was to spit it out in disgust. This church is a classic case of lukewarmness, indifference, and apathy, which was nauseating to Christ. She was unstable in faith and practice like Israel in the days of Elijah (1 Kings 18:21). She was slothful in the Lord's business, like the church at Rome in Paul's day (Rom. 12:11). The Christians at Laodicea needed to drink of the spiritual water of life from Christ to overcome and be rewarded in heaven.

The banking business made the Laodicean Believer rich, but put them in spiritual poverty (3:17a). These great riches filtered into the church and made them arrogant, selfsufficient, and in "need of nothing." They did not realize that they were "wretched, miserable, and poor", spiritually, before God. Christ pleaded with them to obtain from him true spiritual riches. They needed an enrichment of character and attitude before God to prepare for eternity.

Christ described the spiritual nakedness of the Laodiceans in clear contrast to their pride in their garments, which they manufactured from the black glossy wool of the local breed of sheep (3:17b). These expensive robes did not hide their real character before God. Christ told this selfsufficient church to come and obtain a beautiful white robe which would really cover their exposed condition before God (3:18a). White garments would be worn by those willing to repent of this fallen condition.

Laodicea was known for a great medical school and the production of ointment for the eyes and ears, but the church was unaware of her spiritual blindness (3:18b). Their spiritual eyes were blinded to their real condition before God by the wealth, fame, and pride of the city. Christ saw them as selfsufficient, selfsatisfied, selfconfident, and selfcondemned. They needed to buy some eye salve to correct their spiritual vision. They needed the Great Physician!

Christ loved the Laodiceans (3:19-20). He loved them enough to rebuke, chasten, and command them to repent (Prov. 3:12). A definite change was demanded if they were to retain their spiritual standing with God. He was not only trying to scold and condemn them, but wanted to recover their lost souls. He wanted them to be zealous and overcome their fallen condition.

The Christians at Laodicea that were in the process of overcoming would have the privilege to sit with Christ in his throne (3:21). Because the spirit of complacency and selfsufficiency is hard to overcome, Christ offered them one of the greatest blessings. It is the highest honor to share the glory and fellowship with Christ in his throne, which he earned the right to share with his father in overcoming many obstacles. He offered no greater incentive for overcoming.

THE REDEEMED CHURCH

One of the most beautiful pictures in the book of Revelation is the redeemed church (21:1-27). The great question on this section is: Is the holy city, the new Jerusalem John saw, coming down from God, the church, or heaven? There are good arguments for both sides of this question which are forthcoming in this writing.

Why do men say this refers to heaven? Eldred Echols makes a good summary of these arguments in the following list:

1. The first heaven and the first earth are passed away (21:1);

2. There is no more death, sorrow, or pain (21:4);

3. God and Christ are there (21:22);

4. There is no sun nor moon (21:23);

5. The river of life and tree of life are there (22:1, 2);

6. The saved will reign there forever (22:5) (162-63).

These are good arguments. Many of these points are made in the next chapter in reference to heaven where the church is glorified. However, there are some good reasons for believing that the "holy city" John saw coming down from heaven was the church. These arguments present some problems for those who believe that chapter 21 refers to heaven. Eldred Echols also makes a good summary of these arguments in the following:

1. A description of heaven does not fit the context of the prophet's writings on which this text is based (Isa. 30:19; 60:13; 65:17-25; Ezek. 40-48).

2. This city "comes down from heaven" and obviously heaven doesn't come down from heaven.

3. The foundations of this city are the twelve apostles (21:14) which describes the church, not heaven (Eph. 2:20).

4. The gates of this city are still open, and people are coming in and the gates of heaven will be closed at Christ's second coming (21:24-26; Matt. 25:10).

5. The passing away of the old heaven and earth and the coming of the new illustrates the "new creation" of conversion (2 Cor. 5:12).

6. The physical sun and moon do not light the church; Christ is the light (Isa. 2:5; 9:2; 60:1, 3, 19, 20; John 1:9; 8:12).

7. The water of life is salvation through Christ (21:6; Ezek. 47:112; John 4:10; 7:37, 38).

8. The greatest problem people have in applying this section to the church is reconciling 21:4 with this view which is a symbol taken from Isaiah 25:8; 65:17-19. Isaiah gives a description of the healing of the coming messianic kingdom (163-67).

God has planned a new dwelling place for the church. It is logical to accept that John is describing the glorified church in heaven by examining the arguments on both sides of the issue. Heaven and earth will pass away when Jesus presents the church to God (21:1, 22, 23; 1 Cor. 15:24). The redeemed church will not suffer death, sorrow, or pain in heaven reigning with Christ (21:4; 22:5). She will be sustained with spiritual food for eternity (22:12). The overall picture in chapter 21 is the church being made ready for a permanent dwelling place in heaven (21:23).

There are in this context some symbols that describe the church. This is a logical conclusion from other scriptures that refer to the church in the same terminology. John saw "the holy city, new Jerusalem, coming down out of heaven from God" (21:2, 10). He uses Old Testament terms to describe the church which came down to earth as the result of God's plan from the beginning (Eph. 3:8-11). She would be trodden under foot while on earth, but redeemed in heaven (3:12; 11:2; 22:19). The "bride," the wife of the Lamb, reveals the purity of the church made ready for heaven by the blood of Christ (21:2, 9; 19:7; 22:17; Isaiah 61:10; Eph. 5:23-27). The "tabernacle of God" is another Old Testament symbol describing God's dwelling with "his people" in the church (21:3; 7:15; Lev. 26:11f; Ezek. 37:27; 48:35; Heb. 8:2).

God created a new dwelling place for the redeemed man in the church since all evil had been conquered (21:1; 20:11; Isa. 65:17;

66:22; 2 Pet. 3:10-13). John saw an entirely new (*kainos*) city, not an old one renovated for eternity. The word *kainos* denotes something new and unused in quality, in contrast to what is old and out of date. The church is the "new Jerusalem"(21:2) in contrast to the old Jerusalem, which was once the capital city of God's people.

Christ describes the fellowship of the redeemed in the church with God (21:28). She is the "bride" of Christ who redeemed herself from the corruption of Rome, the awful city of the harlot, seen earlier in the book. She is pure from defilement, holy and prepared for a permanent union with Christ (21:27). The "tabernacle" with the mercy seat is an Old Testament symbol of God's presence in the lives of his people, as they are saved by grace through obedience (7:13-17; Exod. 29:45). The lives of God's people, which were once marred by sin, pain, and heartaches, will be made new by a new order of eternal blessedness in heaven separated from the unprepared (21:48). John does not dwell on the lake of fire. His main goal is to describe the glory of the redeemed church.

The church which contains the redeemed (saved) is described in this chapter as a city. John saw the external features of the redeemed church in heaven (21:9-21). The city or dwelling place is prepared as the bride of the Lamb (21:9-10). It is filled with the glory of God (21:11, 23; 15:8; Isa. 60:12; Ezek. 43:2). The abundant entrance into the city is secure with twelve gates (21:12-13). There is no enemy strong enough to penetrate the thickness or scale the height of this glorious city. The city is permanent with twelve foundations (21:14). The unity of God's people from the Old and New Testament dispensations is represented by the symbol of twelve. There is ample room for all the saved in the city that is a perfect cube (21:15-17). John saw a radiant beauty in the foundations, gates, and streets of the city (21:18-21). It is pure and beautiful from the foundation to the top.

The interior features of the city of God are holy (21:22-27). The city has no physical temple (21:22). God and Christ, the Lamb, dwell in the church and in heaven with the saved (1:8; 5:6; 7:17; 14:4). In heaven there will be no special meeting place such as the earthly sanctuary or temple. In AD 70 the temple was destroyed by the Romans and never was rebuilt under God's plan (Matt. 24:1f). It was removed as a place of worship at the death of Christ, and the church was established on Pentecost in AD 33. The church is the temple of God (1 Cor. 3:16-17). It is now seen in heaven; so no place, like the Most Holy Place in the temple, is needed to worship. The saints are present with God and Christ. There is no need for an earthly paradise in a rebuilt temple in Jerusalem when Christ returns at the end of the world.

The city has no physical light or heat (21:23). There is no night there and no sun and moon, for God and Christ provide the light of righteousness for the people of God (Isa. 60:19-22). The glory of God illuminates this heavenly existence (21:11). People from all nations can enjoy these blessings in the New Jerusalem (21:24-26).

The New Jerusalem is more secure than any of the ancient cities (21:25). The ancient cities had to shut their gates at night to keep out the enemy, but no enemy or sin will enter the heavenly dwelling of the church (21:27). This is the reality of the prophecy of the light of God's presence expelling the darkness of the world (Zech. 14:6-9). The church has won the victory over everything that has been hateful and damaging to her earthly existence. This book was a great encouragement to the suffering church.

The church was established and grew in a dynamic way under the Roman Empire. Christ was her Lord. Jehovah was her great overseer and provider. The Holy Spirit moved within her to provide comfort in times of persecution. There is victory in the church. Christ loved the church and cared for the condition in which she stood before God. The letters addressed to the congregations in Asia reveal the character and actions of God, who cares for her spiritual condition and provides for victory within the kingdom of heaven. In the following chapter, I intend to communicate the story of the assembly of the saints' win over all enemies.

Chapter 6

Victory Over Enemies

It is a natural response of any Christian to inquire by what means the children of God can obtain victory over the established religions and kings of the earth. In the heart of the Revelation, John wrote of this victory being in Jesus Christ, the Lamb of God (5:5-6; 17:14; John 1:29). He will conquer Satan, the great harlot, the beasts, and the false prophets (19:19-21; 20:10). The word "overcome" *(nikao)* describes the power God has to prevail (Rom. 3:4) and the ability the followers of Christ have to overcome their enemies through faith in Christ (2:7, 11, 17, 26; 3:5, 12, 21; 12:11; 15:2; 17:14; 21:7). Faith in Christ is the strength to overcome all enemies (1 John 5:4). The saints are more than conquerors.

The prediction of John concerning Christ's conquering these kings of the earth is the answer to the saints' cry for God to take vengeance on their enemies (6:9-10). It ties in with the hope of the Old Testament that God will take vengeance on the enemies of his people (Deut. 32:43; Ps. 58:10; Rom. 12:19-21). The enemies of God shall be consumed (Ps. 37:20; 73:27). Jeremiah knew that God, knowing the mind and heart of the enemy, would take vengeance and deliver his cause (Jer. 11:20; 20:12-13). Likewise, John wrote of the victory of God's people over their enemies.

In the midst of opposition from Satan and the Roman Empire, Jesus Christ was considered the King and Conqueror to every Believer in the New Testament era (17:14b). In the Revelation and to the Jews who expected the Messiah, Christ was King as well as a Prophet, a Martyr, and the Son of God. History relates this wonderful victory story of Believers' respect for Christ, the longed for Messiah, as they were freed from the fetters of the Mosaic Law and came into the New Testament era:

> From the beginning of the world an uninterrupted series of predictions had announced and prepared the longexpected coming of the Messiah, who, in compliance with the gross apprehensions of the Jews, had been more frequently represented under the character of a King and Conqueror, than under that of a Prophet, a Martyr, and the Son of God (Gibbon 147).

TRIBULATION CONQUERED

John was in a period of tribulation with the rest of God's saints at the time of his writing (1:9; 2:9, 22). The word "tribulation" (*thlipsis*) denotes a period of oppression, affliction, and distress which is brought on by external circumstances. Jesus Christ came to conquer these outward circumstances such as war, famine, death, persecution, and judgment (6:18:5). The term "great tribulation" (7:14) suggests a definite period of time spoken by Christ during which Satan would afflict the saints of God with spiritual trouble and anguish (12:13-17; 1 Thess. 2:14-18). This is the period of time that John testified that he shared with the saints when he wrote the book of Revelation.

Jesus Christ came forth to conquer the world with its tribulation in persecution (6:1-11:19). He opens the book with seven seals (6:1-8:5). The vision of the four horsemen reflects on Zechariah's vision of Christ, the Branch, who would bring peace and victory in times of war, famine, and death (Zech. 6:1-15). The white horse is a symbol of conquest in war (6:12). The white color represents victory and prosperity. The bow in the rider's hand represents his power to overcome his enemies which is his mission. This interpretation is based on the prophecy that Christ would conquer in truth and righteousness using sharp arrows (Ps. 45:37). The Son of God came to conquer Satan who is the author of all tribulation in this world (John 3:13-17; Col. 2:14-15).

The "white horse and its rider" represent the victory of the cause of Christ. The figure of horses, a symbol of strength and power especially in war, completes the picture of Old Testament prophecy of the strength of God through Christ to give his people rest in time of trouble (Job 39:19-25; Zech. 1:8-11; Matt. 11:28-30). This is a logical interpretation because nowhere in Revelation does white denote anything but the purity, holiness, and the glory of God and the cause of his people (2:17; 3:4, 5; 4:4; 6:2; 7:9; 19:11; 20:11). God purifies His people in righteousness denoted by the color of this horse.

The horse is also a symbol of war. In the Old Testament, the horses were used in war, such as Pharaoh pursuing the Israelites departing from Egypt (Exod. 14:23-28), David's victories (2 Sam. 8:4; 10:18), and the Israelites in battle against Egypt (Jer. 46:4). In the New Testament, Jesus used a colt, the foal of a donkey, in his triumphal entry into Jerusalem (Matthew 21:27). Therefore, this was a righteous war which began when Jesus ascended to heaven and the disciples began to preach the gospel (Acts 1:8-11). The rider of the white horse wore the crown of victory usually given to a conquering king (19:11-16). The vision explains the victory of the righteous war that will go on between truth and error until Christ returns to destroy the world. The gospel would prevent Rome from standing forever.

Christ came forth to open the second seal, a seal of bloodshed in war because of the red color of the horse (6:34). Practically every Bible student sees this one as bloodshed, carnal warfare, and the desolation caused by the sword. The term "great sword" means the Roman short sword, which was great because of the constant and terrible slaughter it always symbolized and enabled the Roman armies to destroy and conquer. The earth was to be a slaughter house, not a place of peace. Such a sign was given to Jerusalem (Matt. 24:68). Since Christ opened the seal to John on Patmos, many saints have been slaughtered in the wars between righteousness and wickedness which began in the Roman Empire (17:6, 14; Matt. 24: 6). The saints would suffer many wars before the return of Christ.

The Lamb then opens the seal of famine (6:5-6). The "balance," used by the rider on the black horse to measure wheat, denotes a famine. The color "black" is symbolic of distress, woe, and mourning. The "balance" is a figure revealing the cause of the distress, namely, a famine. It is a strict measure or weight (Ezek. 4:16, 17). This is logical because during a famine food is doled out by weight (Lev. 26:26; Ezek. 4:9-10). A day's earnings would buy a very small amount. After the destruction of Jerusalem by the Romans, famine followed as Jesus had predicted (Matt. 24:7). Believers would have to use the commodities of life, such as "the oil and the wine," with great caution. The "black horse" of famine has ridden into many countries and will continue in all generations until the end of time. Famine is devastating, not only to the victims of war, but also to those who cause the war.

The seal of death is opened to afflict people in the fourth part of the earth by the "pale horse" which denotes death and destruction. John gives two keys to understand the meaning of this horse. (1) Death is the name of the rider (6:8). (2) Death and Hades (grave) are seen gathering up their victims (6:8b). The second and third seals revealed death by war and famine; now the king of terrors himself appears and in his cruel hand are gathered all forms of death by war and plague. The Believers should take courage from the opening of this seal because death by military conquest, war, famine, and pestilence are forces that God can also use to deliver his people from their oppressors.

The seal of persecution is opened by the martyrdom of Believers (6:9-11). Christ had already predicted that his followers would suffer persecution (Matt. 5:10-12). The souls of Christians are now seen under the altar of sacrifice for his cause (3:21; 20:4; Acts 14:22; 2 Tim. 3:12). The martyrs died for the Word of God and their testimony for Christ. Many saints died during the reign of Nero and Domitian

(2:13). God is mindful of the death of his martyrs. The altar is a symbol of the saints being, in some sense, in the presence of God, despite their having been slain for the cause of Christ. They are regarded as having been offered upon the heavenly altar.

In the opening of the next seal, God responds to the cry of the martyrs for the punishment of their enemies (6:10-11). God will take vengeance on the enemies of Christianity (Luke 18:7-8; Rom. 12:19); however, he reminds them that the final punishment of their persecutors must wait until the number of martyrs is fulfilled. One is reminded in the book of Romans that "the wrath of God is revealed from heaven against all ungodliness and unrighteousness of men, who hinder the truth in unrighteousness" (Rom. 1:18). Meanwhile, the martyrs are given a "white robe" as a symbol of their purity, pledge of their victory, and absolute assurance of eternal life.

The martyrs are taught to look forward to the final day of judgment (1:12-17). The key to understanding this passage is that "the heaven was removed as a scroll when it is rolled up; and every mountain and island were moved out of their places" (6:14). Peter used similar terms in describing the removal of the heavens in the last day (2 Peter 3:10) when God will judge all men (6:15) through Christ (6:16; John 5:22; Heb. 10:30-31). In reference to the judgment of God in the last day, the question of who will be able to stand (6:17) is answered in chapter seven. You can stand! You have no tribulation that has not been conquered in Christ.

INTERLUDE: SEALING OF BELIEVERS

Jesus Christ reveals to John in an interlude the sealing of the servants of God, which makes the martyrs (6:9-10) able to overcome in tribulation on earth and the final judgment of God (6:17; 7:1-17). Triumph is the last word in the history of the church. Tribulation does not have the victory. Victory is in heaven after the judgment where the martyrs of "the great tribulation" are seen by John (7:13-14). First, God must seal his servants and make a remnant secure from all enemies as he did in the Old Testament history of his people (Joel

2:32). A special note is given to the sealed, the 144,000, and the great tribulation.

The sealing of the servants of God restrains the angels of judgment (7:13). The angels holding the four winds of the earth denote calamity (Jer. 49:36; Matt. 24:31). Their function was that of restraining the destructive forces of the earth until God seals those seeking redemption (6:17). This is in harmony with the limitations placed upon the horsemen of the last seals who could only hurt the fourth part of the earth (6:8). God gave man time for redemption before he destroyed the world in Noah's day (Gen. 5-6). He warned the disciples of Christ to prepare before the destruction of Jerusalem (Matt. 24:12-14). He is preparing the saints now for the fall of Rome and the end of the world (Amos 4:12; Heb. 9:27-28; Rev. 17-18). They must be sealed of God.

One of the great problems in this text is the "seal of the living God" (7:2-3). The word "seal" denotes the right of ownership and security in the form of a designated people (5:19; 6:1-12; 8:1; Ezek. 9:4). It is used in a metaphorical sense referring to circumcision as a seal of righteousness in the covenant that God made with Abraham (Gen. 17:10f; Deut. 10:15-16; Rom. 4:11). Circumcision, called by rabbis the seal of Abraham, confirmed that the seal was by faith and obedience to God's covenant. John had earlier written in his Gospel that what God had sealed or confirmed by the Holy Spirit in man's obedience to Christ was a true witness (John 3:31-36). The work of the Holy Spirit sealed the fact that Christ was the Son of God (John 1:33-34; 6:27). Paul spoke of Christians being sealed in the spiritual things of salvation by the indwelling of the Holy Spirit, certifying that they are the sons of God (Rom. 8:16; 15:28; Eph. 1:13-14; 4:30). The Lord knows those who are his according to this seal (2 Cor. 1:21-22).

The "seal" given to baptized Believers in Christ makes a positive identification of the 144,000 as Christians (7:4-8). Christ seals the righteous remnant of spiritual Israel of God who are identified as "servants of God" (7:3). They are the innumerable multitude from every "nation, tribe, people, and tongue" (7:9) and followers of the

Lamb (7:14). In the interpretation of the 144,000 one must be aware that they are virgin men (14:15) and that the church is the true Israel of God according to the scriptures (21:12; Rom. 9-11; Gal. 3:29; 4:21f; 1 Pet. 1:1; 2:9-10). The number 144,000 represents a complete number of the redeemed from all dispensations, not literal fleshly Jews. It compares with the twentyfour elders (4:4) which included representatives from the Old and New Dispensations. God will not forget anyone who is worthy. We are worthy of eternal victory in Christ.

The innumerable multitude washed their robes in the blood of Christ (7:9-14). The persecuted saints have now been delivered from their enemies by the righteous death in Christ. They have peace and joy, and every sorrow is healed. Therefore, the sealed, the 144,000, and the innumerable host are the same peoplethe saved. John has in view the worldwide, universal nature and victory of the church in heaven after the judgment.

The victory of the saints over their enemies is seen in the "white robes" and the "palms" (7:9). The "white robe" symbolizes the character in which man drapes himself as a result of his righteous deeds and habits. White is heaven's color of immaculate purity and victory. "Palms" suggest that the multitude stands before the throne rejoicing at the close of the harvest (Jer. 8:20). They are rejoicing because of victory over the tribulation on earth that was caused by the enemies of Christianity.

The saints have the victory because of the blood of the Lamb (7:10-14; 1:5; 5:9; 12:11). The blood of Christ is superior to the power of the enemies of Christianity who spilled the blood of the saints. Revelation uses blood to signify this destruction of the saints and the death of their persecutors (6:12; 8:8-9; 11:6-7; 16:36; 17:6). The victory belongs to the saints because the blood of Christ overcame "the great harlot" (Rome) and gave salvation to the obedient (17:5; 18:2; 19:13). The souls seen before the throne had "washed their robes in the blood of the Lamb" in obedience to the Gospel (1:5; Acts 22:16; Tit. 3:5). John uses the metaphor here to show the part that man must play to obtain salvation in Christ.

John saw the souls that came out of "the great tribulation" standing before the throne of God rewarded eternally (7:14-17). This is usually a proof text for the premillennial theory on the Great Tribulation. However, John saw those "that come out of the great tribulation" (7:14). The verb "come out" is a present middle participle meaning "they continue to come." Therefore, the biblical truth is that John speaks of a period of persecution which is going on now in the Christian Dispensation (1:9; 2:9). The interlude reveals that God will remove the tears of such things as anxiety (Acts 20:31), sacrifice (Acts 20:19), pity (Luke 19:41-42), and sympathy (1 Cor. 12:25-26). He wipes away all tears as a father wipes the sorrow and tears from his son's eyes. Praise God for victory!

THE SEVENTH SEAL OF JUDGMENT

The opening of the seventh seal in silence precedes the storm of judgment (8:1-11:18). God accepted the prayers of the saints after the opening of the seal (8:3-4). The saints prayed that God would avenge the blood of their persecutors (6:9-10). The vision contained seven trumpets of judgment on the foes of Christ and his followers symbolized by fire (8:5). The sixth seal (chapter 6) brought a vision of judgment, followed by a special vision of the safety and felicity of the saints (chapter 7). God hears the saints from heaven and responds to their prayers.

The seven trumpets are structured with the same pattern as the seals. The number seven denotes perfection or completion in judgment. The trumpet is a symbol of war, judgment, and last things (Matt. 24:31; 1 Cor. 15:50f; 1 Thess. 4:16). The judgments of the seals were natural, ordinary events, but the judgments of the trumpets were supernatural. The first four trumpets deal directly with the activities concerning the lower creation because they affect the land, sea, fountains, and atmosphere. The last three deal more directly with men, afflicting men with pain, death, and hell. They are called the "woe trumpets." These are judgments on the wickedness in the world which God does not ignore. God is taking action against sin in the severe warnings of the trumpets. The fire coming down with the trumpets symbolizes the fiery judgment of God upon the enemies of his saints in answer to their prayers (6:10; Ps. 41:1-30). The first trumpet blasts a judgment on the land (8:67). The first four trumpets give briefly the active involvement of God in bringing judgment upon the wickedness of man. The book of Revelation is not a "Book of Doom," but one that reveals God's limitation and restraint on the wickedness of man present since man rebelled against his Creator. The plagues of Egypt certainly connect to the first four trumpets in a general way (Exod. 7-11). The point of these natural calamities was that Egypt might know that God rules the universe and he will deliver his people (Exod. 7:5). The Roman Empire could easily get the message that Jehovah is the God of the universe in these first trumpets.

The first trumpet expresses that sin has injured nature itself, for it cries out against man (Rom. 8:18-25). God brings judgment on man intending to lead him to repentance. The "hail, fire and blood" is figurative language expressing the violent and destructive nature of the things foretold. These environmental judgments affect man indirectly. The world has been a struggle for man since the fall in the Garden of Eden. Natural disasters from fire, water, and wind have certainly burned up a third part of the earth, warning man of sin and his need for God. Vegetation suffered greatly from this trumpet. The third part represents a partial destruction. This in all probability was fulfilled in warnings given to the persecutors of the saints under the Roman Empire.

The second trumpet brings a disaster upon the sea and its inhabitants (8:8-9). The destruction of this trumpet reminds one of the first Egyptian plagues (Exod. 7:20-21). God used the sea in Isaiah's day to bring judgment upon wicked nations persecuting his people (Isa. 2:1-22). The judgment brought upon wicked nations reveals that Jehovah still rules the universe. The context of Isaiah 2 is that many idolatrous nations would flow into "Jehovah's house," which is the church (1 Tim. 3:15). Likewise, the vision of great upheavals such as burning mountains and ships on the sea would sound a great warning for the enemies of God's saints such as Rome.

The third trumpet brings a disaster of bitterness upon the rivers and fountains of water (8:10-11). The star is identified as "Wormwood." Wormwood is a woody herb known for its bitter taste, which is symbolic of bitter sorrow, bitter evil, or bitterness of soul (Lamentations 3:19; Jer. 9:15). The vision symbolizes an act of judgment sent on an impenitent world. It is a metaphor which identifies the vision as a divine judgment (Amos 5:7, 6, 12). It affects the very thing that man depends upon for life water. His source of survival and joy becomes his defeat and execution.

The fourth trumpet brought disaster because of abnormal functioning of the heavenly lights (8:12). The vision stands for the heavenly intervention of the atmospheric area of man's environment. The vision, as the ninth plague on Egypt, reveals that a third part of all light will fail. It must be kept in mind as one interprets this symbol that God made the sun, moon, and stars to rule the day and night (Gen. 1:14-19). God has used these heavenly bodies in the past for and against man in battles of judgment on earth in reforming the wickedness of man (Exod. 10:21; Josh. 10:12; Isa. 50:3; Joel 2:10-11, 31; 3:15). It is a symbol denoting tribulation and destruction (Isaiah 13:10; Matthew 24:29; Revelation 6:12; 16:8). The aim of God's action is to deliver a righteous remnant (7:13-17; Joel 2:32; Acts 2:16-22). John saw a period of time during the Roman Empire that God warned sinful man through abnormal functioning of these heavenly bodies to repent. God rules everything in heaven and on earth. Wicked man corrupts the earth through rebellion. The rejection of God's rule causes the tribulation suffered in life.

John reminds his readers in the visions of the first four trumpets that God uses environmental phenomena to bring destruction on the enemies of Christians. Ray Summers gives a good application of these trumpets to the Roman Empire in the following:

> All these are pictures of natural calamity as an agent of
> destruction against Rome, the enemy of the Christian

people. One of the main things that led to the breaking down of the Roman Empire was a series of natural calamities causing disaster over the empire such as volcanic eruption in Mount Vesuvius (August A. D. 79), fiery flood engulfing Herculaneum and Pompeii, ashes from a burning mountain falling on ships and shores of Egypt and Syria, earthquakes, and the sun being blacker and thicker than all nights (156).

The eagle brings an intermission by announcing further woes on the enemies of God's people (8:13). This is an introduction to the woe trumpets that affect man directly. The eagle, a bird of prey, is a symbol of pillage and plunder, characterized by swiftness and strength (Job 9:26). The eagle flying in the direct line of the sun symbolizes the judgment of God being seen and heard by all the inhabitants of the earth.

VICTORY OVER ROME

The amazing thing about empires from the beginning of time up to the present day is they fall. All ancient empires fell: Assyria, Babylonia, Persia, Greece, and the Mongols. "Modern empires are either gone or severely diminished: the Ottomans, the Dutch the British and the Soviet. Among all these empires, the question of why Rome fell excites the greatest interest" (Wolpe 45). Many have falsely guessed in time. They predict it was financial, morality, atheism, cruel and persecuting leaders, and some dare say a caustic picture of Christianity. "On the contrary, Rome fell not because of the betrayal of Christian ideals, but because of their fulfillment" (Ibid 46). I intend to reveal that God planned from the beginning for the removal of Rome as a world powerful kingdom in Christ (11:15). Christ is the King of the last world kingdom!

The fifth trumpet brings destruction on the fallen star (9:1-12). The symbol of a fallen star was taken from Isaiah who pictured the fall of the King of Babylon as a fallen star (Isa. 14:12f). Satan has used notable beings such as Herod to fight Christ since his birth in Bethlehem (Matt. 2:1-33). He fought Satan, the leader of world powers, since his experience in the wilderness (Matt. 4:1-11). The true application of this woe trumpet is the fall of the Roman Empire whose leader was under the influence and leadership of Satan.

Stars usually denote nobility in subordinate princes and great men of both political and ecclesiastical status. Christ is pictured as the "bright and morning star" (22:16). Satan is pictured as a fallen star (Luke 19:17-20; John 12:31). He is the power behind the empire that will lose his nobility. The vision appears at this point in the Revelation to assure Christians of victory over Satan's persecutions.

Satan is given the "key to the abyss." A key is the symbol of authority, which he received from Christ, to open the abyss and incite evil upon men with limitations (1:18; 9:24; 20:1). Satan was allowed to bring natural calamity (flood, earthquakes, volcanic eruption, etc.) upon Rome (8:1-13). He brought internal corruption such as false doctrine, moral corruption to their rulers (9:1-12), and destruction from old and new enemies (9:13-21). God used Satan in the past to bring trials (Job 1:6-12) and false doctrines (2 Thess. 2:8-12) upon man. He now uses Satan to bring woe upon Rome.

The "locust army" is released from the pit with the mission to hurt everyone who is not sealed of God (9:2-10). The locust is a symbol (9:4) of numerous armies of men destroying a country. It is an Old Testament symbol such as the Persians and Babylonians who laid waste Judea (Joel 1:4f). The locust did not feed on vegetation, but on the minds and hearts of men.

The smoke, as a black smoke of a great furnace, goes out into the world. The smoke of deception, sin, moral darkness, and religious degradation kept pouring into the earth from the lowest depravity of hell. The evil influences which Satan used to darken or blind the minds of men are in view.

The conquest of the locust is described with seven characteristics representing a complete destruction (9:7-10). They appear "like horses prepared for war" (cf. Joel 2:4f). They came thundering into the lives of men as wings that carry the echo of a cavalry charge of great speed. They came wearing "crowns" of victory. The symbol of "men's faces" represents the visible forces of Satan with every imaginable, evil, and destructive delusion of hell itself operating in the hearts and lives of wicked men. The "hair as of women" was a mark of certain locust power. The "teeth of lions" was a symbol of fierce and utter destruction. The "breastplates of iron" represent Satan's power to drown the Roman world in defeat. Their "tails" contained the poison to bring spiritual death.

The leader of the invading armies is Satan (9:11-12). The Hebrew name, Abaddon, and the Greek name, Apollyon, identify him as the destroyer. The Hebrew name denotes destruction in the sense of slaying (Exod. 12:23; Jer. 2:30). The Greek name denotes destruction by ruin (Heb. 11:28). Satan is the destroyer of the character, morals, hope, and the very life of man (John 8:44). The message of this trumpet is the destruction of the Roman Empire by the barbarian armies.

The sixth trumpet unleashed a cavalry of 200 million men, which is a symbol of irresistible power (9:13-21). The key to the interpretation of the passage is "the great river Euphrates." The river was 1700 miles long serving as the boundary line between Rome and the Parthian nation. It was a natural boundary and defense for Israel on the Northeast (Gen. 15:18; 1 Kings 4:21). The Parthians are mentioned twice in the Bible: they were a great destructive force on the East (Dan. 11:44) and neighbors with the Medes and the Elamites (Acts 2:9). They were Rome's most dreaded enemy and a constant threat to her eastern border. The vision represents the Parthian cavalry coming from the land of the Euphrates to invade the Roman Empire.

John takes another interlude to assure the faithful children of God of victory in the hour of woe over their enemies (10:1-11:13). The interlude deals with the little book, the temple of God, and the two witnesses. The mighty angels, clothed in the radiance of heaven and the authority of God, are used again in delivering the vision (10:14; 5:2, 14; 6:15; 8:21; 18:1; 20:1). The glory, rank, and authority of God are seen in the whole earth and sea in the message of the little book.

The message of the little book was according to the mystery of God, the Gospel, which was declared to the prophets in the church (10:58). Old Testament prophecy was referred to as a secret or mystery (Amos 3:7). The Gospel is the mystery of God (Rom. 16:25; Eph. 3:4). Prophets were used in the early church to declare the gospel for edification (1 Cor. 14; Eph. 4:11-12). John was given a message in the Revelation of divine retribution and vindication of righteousness in prophecy (1:3).

God told John to eat or digest the message of the book (10:8-11). This symbolic language was taken from Ezekiel, who was given a book containing the Word of God in prophecy and was told to eat or digest the message of hope and victory for God's people over persecuting nations (Ezek. 2:8-10; 3:3; 37:4, 9). The message of the book would be bitter to the disobedient and the unfaithful Christians. However, it would be sweet to the obedient and the faithful Christians. A central part of this message is contained in the Revelation, which is addressed to many peoples, nations, tongues, and kings (5:9; 7:9; 11:9; 13:7; 14:6; 17:14-15). The little book is the gospel as revealed in Revelation, which is a message of victory over the Roman Kings.

The second part of the interlude is a message of the vindication of Christianity through the church (11:12). The vision is similar to the one Ezekiel received where the Old Testament temple was carefully measured before its restoration (Ezek. 40-42). The measuring rod given to Ezekiel was the Word of God contained in the immediate prophecy.

What temple did John see in the vision? It is doubtful that he saw the Old Testament temple because this temple was destroyed in AD 70 in the destruction of Jerusalem and was never rebuilt (Matt. 23:37-39; 24). The present writer gives a later date for the Apocalypse (A. D. 96) in the introduction (p. 2) of this writing. In fact, what meaning and comfort would this temple be to persecuted Believers? Why would John break the context in reference to the Jewish Temple? It would prove nothing. The scriptures teach that the church is the temple (*naos*) of God (1 Cor. 3:16-17; Eph. 2:19-21). John uses the word *naos* meaning the temple over which the Lord God Almighty and the Lamb rule as seen in the Apocalypse (3:12; 7:15; 14:15, 17; 15:5, 6, 8; 16:1, 17; 21:22). The word *hieron*, which never appears in the book of Revelation, describes the Jewish temple in the Gospels (Matt. 24:1; Mark 13:3; Luke 21:5). Therefore, John saw a vision of the church rather than the Jewish temple.

John was given "a reed like a rod" (11:1) to measure the temple. In literal terms John used the words "reed" and "rod" in reference to the bamboo like cane some ten or fifteen feet long carried by a shepherd. The symbol could easily be interpreted in ancient culture as the staff, scepter, or authority of a ruler. The Ruler is Jesus Christ from the tribe of Judah who would rule over the church and the Roman Empire with the word of his mouth (2:27; 5:5; 12:5; 19:15; Gen. 49:10). He will use the Word of God to measure or determine the membership, the altar of sacrifice, worship, work, and character of the church and to defeat the Roman gods.

Otto Kiefer gives an excellent testimony that the rise of Christianity, through the Gospel taught by the church, was a factor in the fall of the Roman Empire in the following:

> It cannot be doubted that, as well as the purely economic causes of the decline of ancient civilization, there were spiritual causes at work, causes usually summed up as 'the rise of Christianity. The old state could not be preserved by a religious attitude to life- an attitude which did not only condemn the Empire and the principate by which it was governed, but set up, in opposition to the existing scheme of human life, the new, almost ascetic ideal of overcoming this world (349-70).

The third part of the interlude is the testimony of the two witnesses (11:3-13). They are referred to as "two olive trees and two candlesticks" (11:4). This part of the vision is similar to the one given to Zechariah of a candlestick and two olive trees standing by its side (Zech. 4:15). The interpretation of this vision was the Word of Jehovah by the

Spirit (Zech. 4:6). The church is the candlestick (1:20). The number two is symbolic of that which has been strengthened or doubled. The two witnesses represent the entire church that has been strengthened by the Lord to testify of the Word of God for 42 months (1260 days), which is the time the temple will be trodden under foot by Rome (11:27). The various ways which Rome persecuted the Christians has already been established in chapter four of this writing.

The root word for witness and testimony is *martur* or martyr. It refers to those who interpret God's counsels during the times of persecution which cost their lives (1:5; 2:13; 3:14; 11:3, 8; 15:5; 17:6). They would speak forth the mind and counsel of God in the form of prophecy as contained in the Revelation (1:3; 11:6; 19:10; 22:7, 10, 18, 19). Missionaries would proclaim the gospel and the rights of God in the Divine retribution in the message of Revelation. In Revelation 15:5, in the phrase, "the temple of the tabernacle of the testimony in Heaven, the testimony is the witness to the rights of God, denied and refused on earth, but about to be vindicated by the exercise of the judgments under the pouring forth of the seven bowls or vials of Divine retribution" (Vine 1143). The message of the two witnesses would devour their enemies with fire (11:5). The testimony they would give to the persecutors was like Elijah who shut up heaven (2 Kings 1; Jas. 5:17). They were like Moses who had power from God to send plagues upon the enemies of Israel (Exod. 7:20).

A time arose when the testimony of the gospel by these witnesses was crushed (11:7-10). The force that crushed the Gospel was temporarily successful. The Gospel was in a crucial stage during the time of this writing. The beast is embodied in the Roman emperors who made war with the church (13:7) and rejoiced over the destruction of her work. One must remember the church may be persecuted, but not defeated (2 Cor. 4:7-15). Rome, like the cities of Sodom, Egypt, and Jerusalem, will be corrected in judgment (11:8). This wicked city will not devour the people of God.

The witnesses were resurrected, glorified, and restored to their work (11:11-13). The power of Rome will be overthrown, which will enable the redemptive message of the gospel to live again with greater triumph. The enemies would recognize that divine power had restored the work of the church. Man cannot forever silence the power of God. Rome only thought they had silenced Christianity. It will arise from the ashes of persecution. God will do His redemptive work on the earth despite His enemies; death being the last enemy defeated through the death and resurrection of Christ.

In the sound of the seventh trumpet John predicts that the kingdom of Rome would be consumed by the kingdom of Christ (11:14-19). Christ's kingdom and its message of evangelism consuming the kingdoms of the world are exactly what Daniel prophesied (Dan. 2:44; 7:14-27). It will reign in the lives of the people of God forever (Luke 1:33; Acts 4:25f). In the preceding interlude, the Christians were given assurance and comfort that God's righteous retribution would come upon the persecutors. This passage contains the song of victory and rejoicing over these dark days. In the following chapters even darker days will come, but victory will be given in Christ.

John now gives his attention to the sins of the Empire and shows the completeness of its destruction (chapters 12-18). In the forthcoming chapters, one is given an overview of the conflict between the church and Rome. It must be kept in mind that every section of the Revelation is designed to help persecuted Believers. There are seven sins denounced in the overthrow of Rome which harmonize with the reasons given earlier in this writing for the fall of the Empire. The word *sin* is used to denote transgression against God and man, a controlling power, and evil works.

The sin of **persecution** against God and his people is led by Satan (12:1-17). The war begins in heaven with God and Satan (12:7-10). Satan is cast out to persecute the people of God beginning with Christ (12:4, 13). The story depicts an age long conflict between good and evil. It deals with the woman and her child, the dragon, the beast, and the false prophet.

The glorious woman emphasizes a close relationship between the church, the people of God, and her Lord, Jesus Christ (12:15). The woman represents the church as fulfilling the purpose of salvation in Christ during the time of persecution (12:10-12). The people of

God in the Old Testament are symbolized as a woman in travail bringing forth Christ into the world (Isa. 54:1; Mic. 4:9 5:5). The New Testament refers to the church in the symbol of a woman who is victorious over her enemies (19:7, 8; 21:2, 9; 22:17; Eph. 5:22-33). The woman is given a crown of victory, which is promised to the faithful church (12:1; 2:10). She is exalted and glorious as the sun (12:1; Eph. 5: 26, 27). She is victorious over persecution in Christ.

The war of persecution is between the son, a man child, of the woman and her seed and the dragon (12:5, 13, 17). The seed of woman is used in scripture to indicate the Christ (Genesis 3:15; Gal. 3:16; 4). He rules the nations with a rod of iron (2:27; 11:1). The struggle in persecution against Christ and his church is apparent in the book of Revelation (12:17; 13:7; 16:6; 17:6; 18:24; 20:9). When Christ is caught up unto God and his throne, the saints rejoice in victory over persecution (12:5, 10; Acts 1:9).

The great red dragon is identified as Satan who persecutes the people of God (12:34, 9). He is cast out of heaven and assumes his role in persecution (12:7-10). The dragon is a symbol of evil and is the ruler of all that is evil, destructive, and opposed to God. He instigates the persecution, but uses evil governments to accomplish the work with the entire world as his goal. It is his wicked purpose to defeat heaven's plan to provide a redeemer for mankind (12:4). The red color denotes the blood of the martyrs who died in the persecution. One is told earlier in scripture that Satan has this ability (John 8:44; Heb. 2:14-15). The seven heads of the dragon declare the completeness of his power. The ten horns reflect his power to destroy. Satan and his angels are definitely a forceful adversary of God's people (1 Peter 5:8f).

The ultimate goal of Satan is to destroy Christ and his followers and to rule the world (12:4). It is hard to read this without thinking of the persecution of Herod the Great seeking to kill the infant Jesus (Matt. 2:16). The church, which is composed of the saved, will have to flee persecution as Mary did in delivering Christ to the world (1:9; 2:9; 3:9).

Satan is the fallen star, along with the kings of the earth that rose up against God and his people (9:1; 20:1f). He is defeated from heaven by the blood of Jesus Christ (12:11-12; Col. 2:14-15). The death of Christ on the cross made Satan unable to make any charge against God's elect (Rom. 8:33-34). The church is nourished and protected in the death of Christ. Satan is unable to destroy the church as a whole and turns to the individual in the preceding chapters (12:17). God has a place of preservation in Christ from persecution for his people.

The individual child of God is enticed by the sin of **blasphemy** through the beast of the sea (13:1-10). The leader who gave the beast his authority is Satan (13:12). He has the same number of heads (wisdom), horns (power), and diadems (authority) as the dragon (12:3). He became an ally to the dragon to make war with the saints, constituting an unholy trinity for the persecution of the followers of Christ. The sevenheaded beast which came up out of the sea is an appropriate symbol for the great enemy of the church, the sum total of all evil.

The beast came out of "the sea," which is "the abyss" (13:1; 9:1; 17:8; 20:1). The abyss is the abode of demons and the lost dead, the dark underworld where the devil is kept (20:3; Luke 8:31). The beast came from Satan, the angel of the underworld. This underworld is described as the abyss of Sheol or sea (depth), especially the abode of the dead in Romans 10:7; Psalm 106:26, and the abode of demons (Luke 8:31). It is the dungeon where the Devil is kept and the Antichrist (11:7; 17:8; 20:31). Abanddon is the angel of the underworld (9:11), which is capable of being sealed (9:1; 20:1, 3) (Bauer 2). The grave is finally defeated.

The beast of the sea stood with the description of the Roman world, the final Gentile dominating power (13:2). The beast is compared to the four world powers that came out of "the great sea" in Daniel's vision (Dan. 2; 7). The four kingdoms were Babylon (lion), MedoPersia (bear), Greece (leopard), and Rome (iron teeth) which arose out of the earth (Dan. 7:48, 17). The Roman kingdom overcame all three earlier kingdoms, and was itself finally overcome by the kingdom of Christ (11:15; 12:10-11; Dan. 2:44; 7:17-28). Satan failed in persecuting the church.

The federal head of the revived Roman Empire received his throne and authority to persecute believers from the dragon. Satan gave the beast his powerful throne (13:2). The word "throne" (*thronos*) refers "to the seat of authority of human kings such as David, Herod, and infernal rulers at Pergamum, which was a center for the emperor cult (2:13; 16:10; Luke 1:32, 52; 2:13)" (Bauer 364-65). God is still on His throne delivering the saints in full victory.

The beast had an injury to one of the heads which was severe enough to kill him, but he recovered (13:3-4, 12, 14; 17:8). Nero committed suicide in AD 68 which gave relief to the saints and a death stroke to Rome. There was a myth, Nero redivivus, circulated that he would return and work through succeeding emperors. The resurrection and broadening of these persecutions were revived by succeeding emperors. The saints in Asia were confronted with a choice between Christ and the emperors. As time passed, the idea that Nero was still alive changed into the belief that he would be resurrected and his image took on superhuman features in the following four ways.

First, the aim of the persecution offered by the beast of the sea was blasphemy (13:5-6). The word blasphemy, the verb (*blasphemeo*), means to speak contemptuously of God by slanderously reporting, which brought great destruction upon the beast and his followers (13:6; 16:9, 11, 21). The beast caused the people to defame the character of God and his saints (13:6-7; 1 Cor. 4:13). The word "tabernacle" metaphorically means those who dwell with God in heaven and on earth (13:6; 15:5; 21:3). "Nero (AD 64) led the way for some of the most exquisite tortures being inflicted on Christians" (M'Clintock and Strong 6:955).

Second, the beast out of the earth brought the sin of **idolatry**. He had the appearance of a lamb and the speech of a dragon (13:11-18). He presented himself as a religious leader and spoke lies which originated with Satan (John 8:44). His mission was to make men worship the beast preceding him who had received a "death stroke"

(13:12-14). This passage reflects the antiChristian attitude of Domitian who demanded the people to address him as "Lord and God." Merril C. Tenney gives an overview of the scholarship of Tacitus, Pliny, Irenaeus, and William Ramsay who taught that the reign of Domitian was such a severe persecution in the following:

> He was an heir to a policy and legislation established by Nero, and sporadically pursued under Vespasian and Titus both of whom had links with Pal., and entertained some fear any movement initiated there. But Domitian, with a sharp eye for treason and enthusiastic for the Caesar-cult justly ranks with Nero as a systematic persecutor. According to Irenaeus (Iren. Her. V. xxx.3), the Apocalypse of John was written during the reign of Domitian and reflected the emperor's anti- Christian attitude (2:155).

Third, the early church could easily identify this character who did "great signs and wonders" to deceive people to worship the emperor (13:13-15). During this time there was nothing new about the counterfeiting of God's miracles in connection with false religions. This type of miracle was known among the priests and prophets in the Old Testament (1 Kings 18:38). Christ, Paul, and John had to deal with this kind of miracle worker under the figure of the man of sin or antichrist (20:7-10; Luke 9:54; 2 Thess. 2:9). This was all a working of Satan who caused an erection of temples and images of the emperor encouraging false worship. Domitian was not beyond using the priests, known as false prophets, to guide and enforce emperor worship in the Roman Empire (16:13-15; 19:20). Fourth, Domitian imposed a mark upon all the worshippers of the beast and persecuted even to death all others (13:16-18). The word "mark" refers to the number 666, which was engraved or stamped on their right hand or forehead (14:9, 11; 15:2; 16:2; 19:20; 20:4). The interpretation of this could easily be recognized by the early Christians because of the stamps on documents and impressions on coins. The number six falls short of perfection expressed by the number seven. In the ancient culture it represented evil. The number 666 is a symbol for evil exalted to its highest power. Domitian represented sin and evil to the greatest cruelty and degradation in forcing idolatry on the people (Summers 175-77).

In the midst of all this sin and persecution, John gave his readers the hope of victory through Jesus Christ (14:1-20). The saints of God receive the name of the Father on their foreheads as they sing the victory song of the redeemed. It is a mark of ownership, allegiance, safety, and loyalty to God. The 144,000 represent the complete assembly of God's saved people. They are now triumphant, encouraged, and faithful. God did not allow Satan to defeat his righteous cause in the lives of his saints. Jesus Christ, the Lamb of God, is standing on Mt. Zion, symbolic of heaven's rewarding the faithful with a crown of victory. The message of Christ in chapter 14 is basically given in the announcements of four angels. The message of the first angel is to encourage the saints to continue to proclaim the Gospel to promote faithful worship to God (14:6-7). The second angel announced judgment upon Rome for her immorality (14:8). The third angel announced eternal condemnation upon those who worshipped the beast and received his mark on their foreheads (14:9-16). The fourth angel announced judgment on the earth (14:17-20). The prayers of the saints have been answered in the judgment God brought against Rome.

The reader is given an introduction to a series of seven plagues poured out of seven bowls in chapter 15. These plagues are executed in the forthcoming chapters. In the preceding chapters the readers were given symbols that pictured the opposing forces of righteousness and evil in readiness for deadly conflict. Symbols are now given to picture the bowls of the wrath of God in the final retribution of the enemies of Christianity (15:1; Rom. 1:18-32). The redeemed are pictured in exaltation giving God the glory, praise, and thanksgiving for judgment brought against their enemies (15:28).

In the Revelation John gives three series of sevens to paint a picture of the complete overthrow of evil and reward victory to the faithful. The seven seals were a message of assurance that God would protect the church during the Roman persecution (4:1-6:17). The seven trumpets revealed partial judgments against the enemies of God's people (8:1-11:19). The seven bowls of wrath gave a message of repentance for Rome to stop persecuting the church, which was refused (15:1-16:21). Therefore, God released full and complete judgment on the empire which began in the lifetime of the first readers of the letters. Christianity prevailed by teaching that Jesus Christ is Lord (17:14).

A complete judgment of the wrath of God is brought on the sin of **false prophecy** (16:1-21). The angels of wrath made an immediate response to the command of God (16:12). They poured out the wrath of God in judgment to bring men in subjection as in the days of Zephaniah (Zeph. 3:8-9). The wrath of God was poured out upon the spiritual and moral pollution of the total human environment which was instigated by Rome. It judged those who worshipped the beast and killed the saints (16:27), the blasphemers (16:10-11), and the false prophets (16:12-16) in the day of recompense and retribution which had come on those who persecuted the saints.

God entered a great spiritual battle with the false prophets and with the kings of the earth (16:13-14). The spirits came from the mouth of the dragon. Satan is a spiritual leader and influence in the kingdoms of the world (Matt. 4:8-10; Eph. 6:10-12); therefore a spiritual battle is at hand. The beast was Satan's force to attack Christianity through the emperors and false prophets. This was the priestly cult that enforced emperor worship (13:11, 14). The dragon, the beast, and the false prophet appear to work miracles by fraud to deceive the saints (16:14; 1 Tim. 4:12). They called together the kings of the earth to summon them to war against God and his people. Jesus Christ is the strength of the saints to win in this battle against Satan (17:14; 19:15; Eph. 6:10).

The spiritual battle of Armageddon was called together in a place called in Hebrew "HarMageddon" (16:15-16). The battle ground was the Valley of Megiddo (9:11; 19:19), which was located between the Jordan River and the Mediterranean Sea about ten miles from Nazareth. The saints could easily relate to this valley because of the many Jewish wars that were fought there (Judg. 5:19-20; 2 Kings 9:27; 23:29). They could readily recognize a destructive battle to defeat Rome in this symbolic name. The place is symbolic of a mighty spiritual conflict in which Christ ultimately will overcome Satan's persecutions of the church.

The fall of the Roman Empire did not happen in the day of the churches of Asia. It is relevant to show that the empire did reach its maximum extent beginning at this time. The churches did receive courage to help them be faithful to Christ, knowing that the end of the empire is coming. However, history records that the Parthians, a Turanian race, came from the "sun rising" or the East, beginning about AD 226 when the Euphrates was dried up, invading Rome with a strong dominion over the empire for nearly five centuries (16:12; 9:14). It was like the time when ancient Babylon fell to the Medes who diverted the Euphrates (Isa. 41:2, 25; Jer. 51:36). The Parthians, which were east of the Euphrates, were the greatest enemies of Rome who had a cavalry that was the most dreaded force among the fighting men in the ancient world. The Teutonic tribes, northern European stock of people including the Germans, finally defeated Rome (AD 476). This put an end to the imperial government, which was expected since the time of Nero, according to Charles Pfeiffer who gives a good historical background of the fall of Rome in the following:

> The empire reached it maximum extent under Trajan (AD 98-117). Dacia, north of Thrace, was incorporated into the empire, as was the portion of northern Arabia known as Arabia Petraea. Armenia and Mesopotamia were temporarily occupied but Rome was unable to maintain these eastern territories… The empire lasted in the west until AD 476 when it fell before invaders from the north. The eastern, or Byzantine Empire, continued however, until the fall of Constantinople (AD 1453), considered by some historians to be the event which marks the end of the Middle Ages (187-88).

John now turns his attention to the destruction of the **immorality** of Rome (17:1-18). The Imperial City is being punished for seducing the nations with fornication (16:19; 17:2). The kings who promoted such immoral activity were defeated by Christ (17:14). The "judgment of the great harlot" is the main point of this context (17:1). The visions in this context give the ultimate victory of righteousness over all the opposing forces through Christ.

The key to the identity of the harlot is the symbol of "Babylon The Great" (17:5). This symbol should be interpreted in view of the early Christians' knowledge of old Babylon in the Old Testament prophets. This cannot be old Babylon, because God used the Medes to overthrow her because of her pride (Isa. 13: 17, 19; Dan. 2:36-39), sorceries (Isa. 47:5, 9), opposition to God (Jer. 50:21-28), rejection of God's Holy One (Jer. 50:29-32), drunkenness with persecution (Jer. 51:5-10), and idolatry (Dan. 4). Likewise, God's saints will overcome the immorality of Rome because of their commitment to the purity taught by Christ (14:4, 8; 16:19; 18:10).

The harlot, sitting on "many waters," is another key to interpret that John saw the immorality of the Imperial City. (17:15). The present writer maintains this interpretation because of the following reasons. First, she has control over the "scarlet colored beast," which is a personification for the kings or emperors of the empire, and is dressed lavishly in the attire of immorality (purple and scarlet) in opposition to God's purity (17:34; 3:5; 7:13-14; 12:12; 16:15; 19:8). Wealth and splendor are her earthly treasures which she relies upon completely (17:4; Matt. 6:1921). Second, in her hand is "a golden cup of abominations" which contains the intoxicating history of her persecutions on the church (17:4; 18:6 Jer. 51:7f). The blasphemous name "Babylon The Great" is written on her forehead (17:3; 13:1, 7, 16-17). Third, fornication is shown in scripture to be a symbol of spiritual adultery and apostasy (Nah. 3:17). Fourth, prostitution was a great public evil among the Greeks and Romans in the beginning of Christianity (Acts 21:25; 1 Cor. 5:1; 2 Cor. 12:21; 1 Tim. 5:20). The abominable practice of uncleanness and fornication was also prevalent among the Jews (Rom. 2:22). Paul, in the book of Romans, testifies that the early Christians were faced with the sins of sexual immorality (Rom. 1:18-32). Therefore, it is apparent that God's saints were in spiritual battle with these sins in the Roman Empire.

John explains the mystery of the harlot who has leadership to come up out of the abyss and go into destruction (17:7-13; 13:10). The seven heads, ten horns, and diadems parallel the dragon (12:13) and the beast (13:1-10). Satan, the authority behind the harlot and her rulers, is influencing many "peoples and nations" (17:12, 15). John has already seen the victory of the saints over the work of Satan through the blood of Christ (12:7-11).

God took vengeance on these kings who warred against Jesus Christ (17:14-18). "There are two keys in this passage to help the saints of Asia to understand their victory over the present world rulers. (1) John uses the word *kepata* for horn, which refers to the description of the corresponding rulers who hate the harlot (17:12, 16)" (Bauer 430). (2) He refers to "the woman" as "the great city" who presently has a kingdom and rules over the kings of the earth (17:18). The main point of the passage shows that Christ is the King and Conqueror in behalf of every Christian during the opposition of Rome (5:6). Christ, the Lamb of God, is standing on Mt. Zion holding the banner of victory when all is said and done concerning the Roman Empire (14:1; 19:11-16).

Sin in Rome brought **economic** failure, which is caused by pride and luxurious living (18:1-24). It brought spiritual failure before God in heaven (18:1). This chapter uses language from the Old Testament in regard to the fall of Babylon to complete the story of the destruction of Rome. This writing will use this opportunity to concentrate on her economic failure. A nation cannot continue to prosper economically with corrupt practices in business life (18:38). The words "merchant" and "merchandise" suggest business life or trade which failed (18:3, 11, 15, 23). God gave the command for this failure because the kings of the earth became rich from immorality and luxurious living (18:9; 14:8; 17:2; Jer. 51:7). For example, Ezekiel gave lust for luxury as the cause for the fall of Tyre (Ezek. 27:9-25). Nations that give themselves to immorality and luxury will not have a strong economy and will inevitably fall. God quickly revealed the fall of Rome because her false pride had reached heaven (18:78). She cannot continue in her efforts to be rich from sin. God's saints will overcome these sins through Jesus Christ.

The kings of the earth mourn the fall of Rome which was built on a strong territorial conquest and trade expansion, and spiritual and moral decay brought destruction in both of these areas (18:9-19). They mourn because their market place for their merchandise has been defeated (18:11). Their gorgeous apparel, embellishments, and riches have perished with the world (18:12-17). They mourn in realization of deception by the sorcery of the harlot (18:21).

Rome, the great city, will fall like a millstone sinking into the sea (18:21-24). John is speaking of what will happen in the future. This is similar to Jeremiah's description of the fall of old Babylon (Jer. 51:63-64). The life of worldly merchants, religious apostasy, and the persecution of God's people will bring her to total ruin. The saints celebrate with the apostles and prophets (18:20). Christ and his followers will celebrate their victory in heaven with great rejoicing (19:1-21).

VICTORY OVER SATAN

It is the nature of apocalyptic literature in eschatological terms to show the defeat of Satan, the power of evil, who afflicts the righteous through demonic and human agents. Revelation chapter 20 plays this role in Christ's victory over the dragon. It must be remembered that Satan is the source of persecution of the saints (2:10; 9:1; 12:9-10, 13; 13:1). He is conquered by the blood of Jesus Christ (12:11; 15:2; John 16:33; 1 John 2:13). The prayer of the suffering saints has ultimately been answered in the binding of Satan (6:9-10). John saw the victory of the martyrs who died as a result of the work of Satan. The dragon is completely bound, and the final battle between God and Satan is coming to a close in the reign of Christ.

The heart of the doctrine known as "dispensational premillennialism" is taken from this chapter. It states that Christ came to earth to establish his kingdom, but when he was rejected by the Jews he established the church, a phase of it as a sort of afterthought, in its place. It is argued, however, that Christ will return before the millennium, raise the dead in Christ, rapture the living saints for the seven years of "great tribulation" on earth, return to set up his kingdom in Jerusalem, and reign for 1,000 years on David's throne from the holy city. It is a doctrine born out of Zoroastrainism (cosmic struggle between the spirit of good and evil) and apocalyptic Judaism. This theory is relevant to this thesis because, if true, it would have robbed the early Christians of a feeling of victory over persecution caused by Satan. A literal 1,000 years would have given them little comfort and hope. It is necessary to show that Christ is defeating Satan rather than being defeated by the rejection of his kingdom, which existed at the time John wrote the Apocalypse (1:9).

In this passage Christ is binding Satan (20:2). There is not one word said about his second coming to the earth to reign and establish a kingdom in Jerusalem to rule on David's throne. The passage says nothing about a bodily resurrection. These elements may be vital to the dispensational view, yet they are conspicuously absent from this narrative. However, the passage does give hope to the suffering saints in the first century. Satan is limited to what he can do to them through persecution. The old serpent, the Devil or Satan, is bound by the angel (20:13). The strong angel who is at least a representative of Christ has already been seen coming down out of heaven to give John the little book (10:1). Christ has the keys of "death and Hades," which denote his authority to open the abyss and imprison Satan (1:18; 9:12). The chain signifies his power to restrain the devil. Christ teaches his followers in the Gospels that he has power to control Satan (Matt. 12:28-29; Luke 10:17-20). Therefore, they could easily interpret this as a message that Satan's power to deceive is limited or controlled by following Jesus Christ.

The binding of Satan refers to the time when God cast Satan out of heaven into Hades, restraining his power until the judgment (20:1; 9:1; 12:7; 2 Pet. 2:4; Jude 6). The word "bound" (*deo*) metaphorically means to bind one in prison, therefore forbidding and limiting his

131

activity. It is the same word used by Paul in teaching the limits that the law of Christ placed on marriage (Rom. 7:14). The Word of God through the Spirit constrained Paul to go anywhere, but to Jerusalem (Acts 20:22). The Word of God limits the activity of Satan during a time of persecution (Matt. 4:1-11). In a relative sense, Satan has been bound or limited since the death of Christ when he instituted the New Testament (John 12:31; Col. 2:14-15). The early Christians needed to know that he might persecute them, but that he could not destroy the church.

The victory over Satan belonged to those who did not worship the beast and had part in the first resurrection (20:4-6). The "mark" was a seal of consent to the emperor worship in contrast to the seal of identity given to Christians (7:3; 13:16-18; 14:9-10; Gal. 6:17; Eph. 1:13). The Premillennialists who argue for a bodily resurrection of these martyrs forget the symbolic use of the word resurrection in scripture (Exod. 37:12; Rom. 6:4-5; Eph. 2:1, 4-6; Col. 2:12-13; 3:14). Christ spoke of salvation as a resurrection (John 5:24-29). Therefore, the first resurrection represents the salvation and the triumphs of the persecuted saints during the Roman persecution.

The martyrs are comforted during "a little season" or a thousand years (20:7-9). In interpreting these symbols, one must keep in mind that Satan has been cast out of heaven, bound in Hades for a little season or time, and released to deceive the nations for a thousand years (9:1; 12:7). This writer maintains that the little season is the Christian Dispensation for five reasons. (1) The text speaks of the thousand years as a little time (20:3). (2) One thousand years is brief in God's sight (Ps. 90:4; 2 Peter 3:8). (3) In the text Christ is coming down to earth to limit Satan's power which he did in his ministry and death (20:12; Matt. 4:1-11; Col. 2:14-15); then at the close of this time, which is a thousand years (short time), Satan is loosed to deceive the nations (20:3, 7-8; 12:9; 13:14). (4) During this time Satan, through Gog and Magog, representatives of evil nations, imprisoned and brought great tribulation on the saints (1:9; 2:10; Ezek. 38:2; 39:1, 6). (5) The faithful martyrs lived during this time, and the rest of the dead lived with Christ at the close of the thousand years while Satan was cast into fire and brimstone forever (20:4-10; Matt. 25:41; 2 Pet. 2:4). That being the case, it is appropriate to say that the thousand years is the gospel age. In the context of the book of Revelation the time is at hand for the saints to believe and speak the word of God (1:3; 19:10; 22:7, 10).

In context the thousand years is the time between the coming down of the angel to bind or cast Satan down to the abyss and his final overthrow in the lake of fire forever (20:1-10). John teaches in his Gospel that Christ cast Satan down during his earthly ministry (John 12:31-33). The adverb "now" designates the immediate present time in which he would cast Satan down by his death on the cross (John 12:27, 31). It follows that the thousand years must be the time from Christ's death on the cross and his second coming which is the Christian Dispensation. The main thrust of chapter 20 is the overthrow of the devil, the beast, and the false prophet (20:9-10). These are the enemies of Christ and his followers. In the end of all things fire will come down from heaven and seal their eternal destruction. In the meantime, Hades, represented by "the lake of fire and brimstone", will hold their souls (20:10, 14-15; 19:20). These enemies of God's people are in Hades awaiting the judgment when Christ destroys the last enemy of the saints, which is death.

In the judgment of Christ, the last force of Satan is destroyed, which is death (20:11-15). The kingdom is delivered to God, the rule and authority of Satan is abolished, and his power over death is cast into eternal destruction at the end of the world (1 Cor. 15:24-28). Christ will bring "to naught" Satan's power of death (Heb. 2:14-15). Christ has the keys of death and hades (1:18) which he will use to unlock the realm of death and let the dead come forth (John 5:28-29) in his resurrection (2 Tim. 1:10). Death and Hades will finally be destroyed on that great day when both the great and the small will be judged by Christ (20:11f).

The saved will have no fear of eternal death at the second coming of Christ because it has been defeated (1:7). Death will be abolished or rendered of no effect in the death and resurrection of Christ (2 Tim. 1:10). Death and Hades are ultimately powerless, as are all other evil forces (20:1415). The followers of Christ will not experience death after the resurrection (Luke 20:34-38). The saints are admonished to be faithful unto the final defeat of all evil forces.

Ultimately, Christ wins! He begins to close the message of the book of Revelation. The saints of God are standing on the shores of time wavering the victory banner shouting "Praise God, We Won!" "Come, Lord Jesus!" I intend to convey this awesome triumph in the final chapter, so all Believers can join the victory dinner and join the chorus to sing, "Victory In Jesus!"

Chapter 7

Victory At The Parousia Of The Lord Jesus

John, in the writing of the Revelation of Jesus Christ, opened and closed the book by inviting the coming (*parousia*-presence) of our Lord Jesus Christ (1:7; 21:20). The Second Coming of Christ will be a great victory for the suffering saints. One of the last things that Jesus promised the twelve disciples was that He will return (John 14:1-6). In this promise the saints are assured of His presence during the trials and persecutions of the world (1:9; John 16:33). The disciples feared never seeing their Lord again once He ascended into heaven, but this promise comforted that fear of loss. He continues to keep this promise as He opens and closes the last book of the New Testament. In the beginning and the end of the Revelation, the Believers are waving the white banner of victory as the enemy is conquered through Christ.

The apostle Paul comforted the Thessalonians concerning the Second Coming of Christ. He wrote: "For the Lord Himself will descend from heaven with a shout, with the voice of the archangel and with the trumpet of God, and the dead in Christ will rise first. Then we who are alive and remain will be caught up together with them in the clouds to meet the Lord in the air, and so we shall always be with the Lord. Therefore comfort one another with these words" (1 Thess. 4:16-17). It is an awesome comfort and joy to know that we can always be with the Lord! In like manner, Jesus comforted the suffering saints with His promise to return in the clouds in the Revelation (1:7). Paul wrote the book of 1 and 2 Thessalonians with the promise of the Second Coming of Christ to exhort and warn the believers to not be deceived by the false teachers of the day who delighted in distorting the teaching about the return of the Lord (2 Thess. 2:1-3). He proclaimed: "Be not quickly shaken in your mind!"

Believers today are living between two advents of our Lord Jesus Christ. The first coming of Christ is a matter of history. Matthew wrote: "Now the birth of Jesus Christ was as follows: when His mother Mary had been betrothed to Joseph, before they came together she was found to be with child by the Holy Spirit. She will bear a Son; and you shall call His name Jesus, for He will save His people from their sins" (1:18, 21). Christ came as the Savior of the world. The Second Coming of Christ is a matter of prophecy. John wrote: "If I go and prepare a place for you, I will come again and receive you to Myself, that where I am, there you may be also" (John 14:3). "BEHOLD, HE IS COMING WITH THE CLOUDS, and every eye will see Him, even those who pierced Him; and all the tribes of the earth will mourn over Him. So it is to be Amen" (1:7). "He who testifies to these things says, `Yes, I am coming quickly.' Amen. Come, Lord Jesus" (22:20). Therefore, the New Testament opens and closes with the coming of Jesus Christ. Jesus emphatically teaches the Second Advent by saying, "So it is to be Amen!"

It is estimated that one out of every twenty-five verses in the New Testament refer to the Second Coming of Christ. Most of these passages are in the writings of the apostle Paul. In this writing a comparison will be made with the writings of Paul and John concerning the *Parousia* of Christ. Paul wrote: "Now we request you, brethren, with regard to the coming of our Lord Jesus Christ and our gathering together to Him, that you not be quickly shaken from your composure or be disturbed either by a spirit or a message or a letter as if from us, to the effect that the day of the Lord has come" (2 Thess. 2:1-2). The Second Coming of Christ is emphatically taught by Paul and John. The believers in Paul's day could still expect the coming of their Lord. They will be delivered to Him on that day being rewarded for their righteousness!

THE PAROUSIA OF CHRIST

"The primary meaning of the Greek word *Parousia* means the presence, coming, and advent of Jesus Christ peculiar to both Paul and John's writings in 2 Thessalonians 2:1, 8 and 1 John 2:28" (Bauer 635). The term is used in reference to the return of Christ in revelation and manifestation to the world. "In some passages the word gives prominence to the beginning of a period of time which He will be with His disciples such as in the resurrection (1 Cor. 15:23; John 5:28, 29; 1 Thess. 4:15; 5:23), and then with others as at the conclusion of His coming at the end of the age according to Paul in 1 Corinthians 15:24 and 2 Thessalonians 2:8" (Vine 111). The most common dictionary meaning of this word "include the presence of persons or things, the position of planets, arrival, coming, advent, and visit" (Liddel and Scott 1343). In the English usage, we understand the word *Parousia* as the presence of the Lord, which means the state or fact of the presence of a divine or supernatural being such as the coming of Christ.

The word *Parousia* is employed twenty-four times in the New Testament for the Lord's coming. Of this number it is used thirteen times in the Pauline Epistles. It is a technical term for the end-time coming of the Lord. The noun form comes from the Hellenistic Greek. The Hebrew language does not have a comparable noun (Plevnik 5). The Greeks understood this term to mean the benevolent presence of God and Christ though they did not express it much in writing. The noun form of the word was employed to express the image of Christ's coming, which is described in the papyrus texts of the Hellenistic Era. The Ptolemies of this period used the term to refer to the epoch-making events in visits of kings and emperors to a particular city. Upon these visits the citizens made preparations for a glorious event, minted coins to commemorate it, and counted the years for the new age from that time onward. The saints also with this understanding were taught to make preparation for the Second Coming of Christ (1 Cor. 15:23, 58). The Latin equivalent is *adventus* in reference to the coming of an emperor (Ibid 6). This background provided a ready imagery for the depiction of the coming of Christ for the audience of the writings of both John and Paul. However, the coming of Christ is greater in appearance, judgment, defeating sin, and rewarding righteousness than any of the emperors in the day of Paul and John!

The word *Parousia* as a technical term has been developed in two directions: First, the word served as a cult experience for the coming of a hidden divinity, who makes his presence felt by a revelation of his power, or whose presence is celebrated in the cult. Second, it became the official term for a visit of a person of high rank such as kings and emperors visiting a province like Asia Minor and Thessalonica (Bauer 635). In like manner the term is applied to the Messianic Advent of Christ as One of high rank in glory to judge the world at the end of this age (2 Tim. 4:1-4). Paul speaks of this Advent as "the day of our Lord Jesus Christ" when the saints will be confirmed in their faithfulness and "the lawless one" will be brought to an end (1 Cor. 1:8; 2 Thess. 2:8). Therefore, these technical expressions can approach each other closely in meaning, or even coincide with one another. However, the cult experience only provided an understanding of the people of one coming again such as Deity in the presence of Christ.

There is a close connected meaning to the Second Coming and the Revelation of Christ by comparing John and Paul. The concept of the coming of Christ is expressed in the New Testament by some synonymous terms. A. T. Robertson does a great study of these Greek terms in the following:

Parousia lays emphasis on the presence of the Lord with his people, epiphaneia on his manifestation of the power and love of God, apokalupsis on the revelation of God's purpose and plan in the Second Coming of the Lord Jesus. The Lord will at that time gather His people together to forever be with the Lord thereafter (II Mac. 2:7; I Thess. 4:15-17; II Thess. 2:1; Heb. 10:25 (Robertson 47).

The term *Parousia* has been established as meaning the presence of our Lord in the Second Coming. The synonymous term *epiphaneia* was a common term in the Koine Greek used to express a visible appearance of a deity either in person or in some other manifestation of power which Paul used many times (2 Thess. 2:8; 1 Tim. 6:14; 2 Tim. 1:10; 4:1, 8; Tit. 2:13). The audience was drawn to an actual presence of the return of Christ in person. The verb *phaverow* is used four times in Paul, John, and Peter's writings to express the actual manifestation of the coming of Christ (Col. 3:4; 1 Pet. 5:4; 1 John 2:28; 3:2). The general term for the coming of Christ is the verb *erxomai* meaning "to come quickly" (1:7; 2:5; 3:11, 20; 22:7, 12, 17, 20). The predominantly used eschatological term for the coming of Christ to deliver salvation and judgment is *heko* meaning "to come or to be present" in relation to time and events (2:25; 18:8; John 2:4; 2 Pet. 3:10). In the metaphorical sense, it refers to one coming in calamitous times to destroy evil. The word *apokalupsis* identifies the eschatological coming of Christ to unveil, disclose, and reveal His presence (1:1; 2 Thess. 2:3, 6, 8). The Second Coming of Christ will be a true unveiling of His true glory and nature!

THE BACKGROUND OF THE PAROUSIA

The Jews had some idea of the *Parousia*. The two books of Machabees, a Hebrew word meaning "Hammer", as given to Judas because of his bravery in battle against the oppressors of the Jews in the reign of Antiochus IV of Syria (175 BC), testifies to the fact that they believed the Lord would come and gather them together to give them mercy and deliverance. It is recorded: "And when Jeremias perceived it, he blamed them, saying: 'the place shall be unknown, till God gather together the congregation of the people, and receive them to mercy. And then the Lord will show these things, and the majesty of the Lord shall appear, and there shall be a cloud as it was also showed to Moses, and he showed it when Solomon prayed that the place might be sanctified to the great God" (2 Macc. 2:7-8). This gave some background to Paul's admonition of the saints "gathering together to Him" at the appearing of Christ (2 Thess. 2:1). It would be comforting to suffering saints to look forward to being with Jesus!

The Old Testament presents mingled prophecies of the First and Second Advents of Jesus Christ. The term *Parousia* does not appear in the Hebrew or the Septuagint. However, it does appear in those apocryphal books that were originally written in Greek, but always in the singular sense (Jud. 10:18; 2 Macc. 8:12; 15:21; 3 Macc. 3:17) (Tenney 601) The first reference of the Second Coming is one depicting the return of the Lord in captivity to deliver His people (Deut. 30:3). The Jews expected the Lord to return and restore their fortunes which culminated into the disciples of Christ's expectations (Acts 1:6-8). Walvoord summarizes the typical Old Testament prophecies of the Second Advent in the following:

> The OT seldom pictures the Second Coming per se, but often dwells upon the circumstances of the Second Coming, such as the preceding regathering of Israel to the land (Jer. 30:3; Amos 9:14, 15), and the results of the Second Coming-the judgment of the nations (Isa. 2:4), deliverance of Israel (Jer. 31:28), and a kingdom of righteousness and peace on earth (Ps. 72:7) (Ibid 325).

The New Testament has many references to the *Parousia* in eschatological and theological connotation which reveals the Jew and Gentile understanding of this term connected to the Second Coming of Christ. In literature outside the Testaments the word does not occur in the writings of Philo. However Josephus uses it in reference to the presence of God as a Helper, but without any eschatological meaning. Tenney gives the following perspective of the people at the time of the New Testament that a prevailing expectation of the coming of the Messiah was known:

> The Hebrew nation had been established and preserved by the mighty manifestation of Yahweh on behalf of His people and the Jews confidently looked forward to a future divine manifestation with the coming of the Messiah. The nature of these Messianic hopes was not uniform; political, ethical, and apocalyptic elements mingled in the expectations. They looked for the coming of the Messiah in history, but that coming was not without eschatological implications. (Ibid 601)

THE ESCHATOLOGICAL COMING OF CHRIST

The eschatological (final events) return and coming of Christ is a prominent theological theme in all of the New Testament, especially in the writings of Paul and John. These authors knew that Christ had already come to achieve the redemption of lost man through the death on the cross and the resurrection (20:5, 6; Col. 2:13-15; 2 Tim. 1:10). They also expected the return of Christ to consummate His redemptive work that was done while on earth. What do the writings of Paul and John actually teach concerning the Second Coming of Christ? What do they say that is the same? What do they say differently? These questions will be answered and understood by looking exegetically at the term *Parousia*. It is interesting and educational to compare two or more New Testament writers on the same subject.

The attention is turned to Paul first because he was the earliest writer of the two being compared. He used the term *Parousia* thirteen times with significance to this study in the New Testament excluding the book of Hebrews which is questionable as Pauline. He used it four times in reference to the visiting or coming of various personalities to the church at Corinth (1 Cor. 16:17; 2 Cor. 7:6, 7; 10:10). He used it twice concerning his visit to the church at Philippi (Phil. 1:26; 2:12). In all of these passages the audience expected the presence in person of the one who is coming. Likewise, Paul used this term to refer to the actual presence of Christ in the Second Coming (1 Thess. 2:19; 3:13; 4:15; 5:23; 2 Thess. 2:1, 8, 9). The primary meaning of the term in these passages is the being alongside of like a companion and the actual presence of Christ. Paul had his audience to understand and expect the actual coming, advent, or arrival of Christ. He uses one of the synonyms of *Parousia,* discussed earlier in 2 Thessalonians 1:7-10, in the coming of Christ in judgment. He stated that Christ will be "revealed (*apokalupsei*) from heaven with His mighty angels in flaming fire" (1:7). Peter helps one to understand that "the flaming fire" will burn up the present earth at the return of Christ (2 Peter 3:10). Time as we know it will be no longer!

The apostle John only used the term *Parousia* one time in reference to the coming of Christ. He wrote: "Now, little children, abide in Him, so that when He appears (*phaverotha*), we may have confidence and not shrink away from Him in shame at His coming (*parousia*) (1 John 2:28). He used a synonymous term (*phaverotha*) with *Parousia* and *apokalupsi* which is translated "appear" teaching the actual appearance of Christ in person. All of these terms are used synonymously in the New Testament to mean manifestation, uncovering, laying bare, revealing, appearance, or revelation which expresses the coming presence of Christ (cf. Rom. 8:19; 1 Cor. 12:7; 2 Cor. 4:2). In comparing Paul's writing to John, the word *apokalupsis* is translated "coming" to denote the "revelation" of Jesus Christ in the Second Advent.

In context of 1 John 2:28-3:3, the author is discussing the future appearing of Christ in the Second Coming. The admonition is to remain in Christ with boldness at the coming of the Redeemer. There is no question about this reference teaching the return of our Lord, as noted by many scholars and emphasized in reading the following by Stott:

> Some commentators have suggested that the vivid expectation of the parousia in Paul's letters has been replaced in the later writings of John by the coming of the Spirit and the present enjoyment of eternal life. Such a theory either ignores the teach- ing on the second coming which occurs in this letter or dismisses it as an assumption. No: the doctrine of the Lord's return was part of the primitive apostolic faith. Four words (in verbal or substantive form) are used by Paul to describe it – his coming (paraousia), appearing (phanerosis), epiphany (epiphaneia), and revelation (apokalypsis). Of these John uses the first two in this verse. There is ample evidence in the papyri that in the East at that time 'the word (paraousia) was the usual expression for the visit of a king or Emperor' (Brooke). Parousia means literally 'presence', and the personal presence of one now absent, the visible appearing of one now unseen (Stott 121).

The theological doctrine of the Second Coming of Christ is too important to simply ignore. The word *Paraousia* does not appear in the Gospel of John, but he wrote many things about the Second Coming of Christ using other companion terms (John 14:1-6). The disciples of Christ needed reassurance of His coming again after He had explained His going to the Father's house. Philo in his writings refers to this as "the paternal house" (Philo 1:256). The coming of Christ was a great comfort to the disciples and those outside the New Testament. The language he used in this passage is similar to that Paul used in 1 Thess. 4:13-17. Paul and John taught some of the same things concerning the *Parousia* of Christ. Talbert gives a wonderful comparison of these two authors in the following:

1 Thessalonians 4:16-17	**John 14:3**
The Lord will descend from heaven.	I will come again.
We shall be caught up to meet the Lord.	I will take you to myself.
We shall always be with the Lord. (Talbert 204).	Where I am you will be

John agrees with Paul on the fact that Christ is coming back in person (cf. 1 Thess. 4:16; Rev. 1:7; 22:20). The two authors teach that He will return in the clouds with a visible coming (1:7; 1 Thess. 4:17). These writers mention that people will react to the Second Coming of Christ in one of two ways: first, some will have hope, boldness, and a reassurance of their faith (1 Thess. 4:13-14; 1 John 2:28); and second, some will fall away from the faith in the presence of the Lord (1 John 2:28; 1 Cor. 15:23, 58). Believers are encouraged not to "shrink" from Christ, but continue in Him today through great confidence of salvation at the judgment (6:12-17; Phil. 2:9-11)! John and Paul both use a companion word of *paraousia* such as *erxomai* to denote the coming or return of Christ, that is to make an appearance in public (1:7; 2:5; 3:11, 20; 22:7, 12, 17, 20; John 5:28). "The idea of His coming is even plainer in connection with the coming of the Son of Man from heaven, the return of Jesus from His home in heaven in the future sense according to Paul in 1 Corinthians 4:5; 11:26; 1 Thessalonians 5:2, and 2 Thessalonians 1:10" (Bauer 311).

The book of Revelation does not use the phrase the *Parousia* of Christ, but provides a very comprehensive study of the Second Advent of our Lord Jesus Christ. The title of the book uses one of the synonyms (*apokalupsis*) of the word under consideration to mean to *uncover* or *reveal* the presence of Christ in a message to the seven churches of Asia, in order to bring corrective judgment upon them to prepare them for salvation at His coming (1:1). John describes the Second Coming in chapter 19 of this great book as victorious to the followers of Christ. "The obvious implication is that the Second Advent is the crowning event promised by Christ climaxing human history, paralleling in the importance of the First Advent in Revelation 2:10 and 4:4" (Tenney 327). This is also similar to Paul's writings because he used the word *apokalypsin* referring to the *Parousia* of Christ in judgment, which the creation and the sons of God have been longing for (Rom. 2:5; 8:19). In this passage the creation is waiting for the revealing of the children of God in the righteous judgment of Christ. Paul says nothing in this passage about a restoration of the creation back to the Garden of Eden order such as a Paradise on earth.

Many scholars promote the doctrine of a new order of creation, one of peace and tranquility, on earth when Christ returns to establish the new heaven and new earth (Isa. 11:6-7; 65:25; Rom. 8:18-25). Arnold presents this argument in the following very well:

> The Bible's description of the new earth and new heaven uses categories that hark back to the Garden of Eden. The Tree of Life will bear 12 different types of fruit year around, one for each month, and its leaves will heal the nations (Rev. 22:2). There will be no need for temple or sacrifices, sun or moon, because God's presence will provide all that is needed. The Bible ends as it began, with a luscious garden in which God rules supreme and his people enjoy him forever (Arnold 104).

The sure way of getting a proper understanding of Paul's teaching concerning the "creation" is to look at the Greek. What did the present audience hear when Paul used the word *ktisis*? The following Greek scholars present some beautiful and educational ideas for the first century and modern day audience:

> It is the act and process of creation such as the world (Rom. 1:20). Paul refers to that which is created as a result of that creative act such as individual things, created beings (Rom. 8:39; Col. 1:15, 23). The Christian is described by Paul as a new creature

(2 Cor. 5:17). The meaning of ktisis is in dispute in Rom. 8:19-22, though the passage is usually taken to mean the waiting of the whole creation below the human level (animate and inanimate). Therefore, a sum total of everything created, creation, world even civil authorities.(Bauer 456-7).

The primary meaning is the act of creating or the creative act in process (Rom. 1:20; Gal. 6:15). Like the English word it also signifies the product of the "creative" act, the "creature" with a significance to mankind as in Mark 16:15; Rom. 1;25; 8:19 Col. 1:15, 23. The reference is to the creative act of God, whereby a man is introduced into the blessing of salvation, in contrast to circumcision done by human hands, which the Judaizers claimed was necessary to that end (2 Cor. 5:17) (Vine 137).

The creation itself. It is the hope of creation, not of the Creator. Nature possesses in the feeing of her unmerited suffering a sort of presentiment of her future deliverance (Robertson 375-76).

Paul refers to a framing, a founding, a creation, the act of creating the material universe (Rom. 1:20, 25; 8:39; 2 Pet. 3:4), and the human race (Mark 16:15; Rom. 8:19, 20, 21, 22). Hence, a spiritual creation (2 Cor. 5:17). It also denotes an institution and ordinance in 1 Pet. 2:13 (Green 106-7).

The New Testament word *ktisis* does mean the creation in which mankind and Christians are included. The expectation of the Jews and Gentiles of the Second Coming of Christ is broad enough to include everything that God has created, but not many see such a wide meaning here. This makes it probable that Paul means the whole of sub- personal creation. The angels that God condemned are not looking forward to the coming of Christ for they are in hell for an eternity (2 Pet. 2:4). The believers in this passage are distinguished from the whole creation in Romans 8:22-23 (Morris 320). The expectation in this context embraces the whole of creation in a spiritual sense. Paul and John articulate together in presenting the hope of Christians in heaven (Rom. 8:24-25; Rev. 21 and 22) taking place at the return of Jesus Christ. N. T. Wright makes a good case that the expectation of the Jewish apocalyptic in light of Jesus expressing a wider hope in the specific belief in a future resurrection in a new heaven and earth without need of a temple, sun or moon which is the reality of the heavenly world (661).

In order to get a correct biblical view of the order of creation at the Second Coming of Christ, one must begin with Paul discussing the ascending of the saved into heaven (Rom. 10:6). Second, Paul is discussing the "glory to be revealed" to the children of God in the Romans 8 passage, not the reordering of the creation. The "sons of God" are to be revealed at this time (Rom. 8:18-19). This sets the tone for his context. Third, Peter who is in total agreement with Paul, teaches that the present heaven and earth will be "burned up" being "reserved for fire" at the coming of Christ before the establishment of the "new heavens and a new earth" (2 Pet. 3:7-18). The present earth will be destroyed! The Second Coming of Christ is a Day of Judgment and destruction, not a restoration of the present circumstances! Fourth, John is writing a book filled with signs and symbols in the Revelation (1:1). He is not discussing a literal New Jerusalem in Revelation 21 and 22, but a spiritual dwelling for the redeemed church wherein righteousness dwells. The "first heaven and earth passed away" (21:1; 2 Pet. 3:10). John and Peter uses the word *parerchouai* for "passed away" meaning to come to an end or disappear (Bauer 631). The earth as we know it will no longer exist! Therefore, "the tree of life" would be figurative of the healing of the saved who survived the trials and persecution on earth (22:2, 3). The earth and creation will be healed of any "curse." Their groaning as expressed by Paul will cease!

The saved are in a new spiritual place. The sky, the first earth, and the sea are gone, that is, they did not exist any longer. The children of God and the creation can now rest in peace, hope, and victory. The same deliverance that released men from the present suffering and persecution will deliver the creation from the bondage of corruption. Paul taught a transformation of the natural body into a new and glorious spiritual body which will shed light on the old material creation with the appearance of a new spiritual creation (21:1-3f; 1 Cor. 15:42-58). This is all in the context of the Second Coming of Christ (1 Cor.15:23). The creation of the world and the spirit of man are subjected to hope.

The Second Advent of Christ to reward the faithful and judge the wicked is described by John as an awesome event (19:11-21). John is allowed to see into heaven (19:11) and view the victorious Christ coming as a warrior riding "a white horse" (symbolic of victory) down the streets of cities he has conquered. The war is over when Christ returns; it is a victory march followed by the saints of God! The appearance of our Lord is awesome (19:12)! He comes to "judge" with the "Word of God" which He will use to judge the world in the last day (9:11 13; John 12:48). The words of His mouth will strike the "nations" (19:15). He makes use of the "angels," a definite reference to the swift coming of the Lord (8:13; 19:17; Matt. 25:31f). This is a picture of a Jewish king and a Roman Emperor coming in judgment upon a nation he desires to conquer (1 Sam. 17:44-45; Jer. 12:9f; Ezek. 39:17f). The kings of the earth and their armies are defeated (19:16, 18, 19). The "beast" (world political leader), the false prophet, the world religious leaders, and Satan will be thrown in hell forever (19:20-20:1f)! Praise God, the suffering Believers win over all persecution and enemies!

THE SON OF DESTRUCTION AT THE PAROUSIA

One of the greatest comparisons on the *Parousia* of Christ between Paul and John is the coming of the "son of destruction" or the "beast" (2 Thess. 2:1-12; Rev. 13). Paul denies that the Second Coming of

Christ had already taken place at the time of his writing (2 Thess. 2:1-2). He does present the Second Coming of Christ to judge the world as a fact at the end of the age. The "day of the Lord" is the day which God appoints for Christ to reveal Himself as Conqueror (19:11f; 2 Thess. 2:2). This phrase is used many times in the New Testament to denote the time, which no one knows, for the return of Christ, but Paul did not want the Thessalonians to be deceived into thinking that this day had already taken place because the circumstances in this context must first become a present reality (Matt. 24:36; 1 Thess. 5:2-3; 2 Thess. 2:2, 3).

There are many great parallels of the "son of destruction" in Paul compared to the "beast" in John in the two passages mentioned above. First, the "apostasy" or rebellion against God and righteousness must take place (13:6; 2 Thess. 2:3). Paul and John expected many great uprisings of political power and evil against God (13:7; 1 Tim. 4:1-3; 2 Tim. 3:1-9; 4:3-4). Second, the man of sin, destruction, or lawless one must appear, who was already at work when Paul wrote to the Thessalonians (13:1, 5, 16, 18; 2 Thess. 2:3, 7). He is the one who causes destruction, ruin, or loss to the saints of God. Third, the one under discussion is "a man" (*anthropos*) meaning a human being (13:5; 2 Thess. 2:3). Fourth, he opposes and exalts himself against God to the defying of worship (13:6, 8, 10; 2 Thess. 2:4). Fifth, his coming and work is according to the power of Satan (13:2, 4; 12:9; 2 Thess. 2:9-12). Satan is the source of all evil work against believers (12:9; 13:7). He will deceive many by concealing the truth of salvation in unrighteousness. Sixth, he was "displaying himself as God" (13:8, 15; 2 Thess. 2:4). These two New Testament writers are reminding their believing audience of the uncertainty in the world at the time of the *Parousia* of Christ. The "son of destruction" is personified in a line of persecuting Roman Emperors, especially Nero in Paul's day and Domitian in John's time. In fact, Domitian was known as "Domitian the God!" However, the passages teach the Second Coming of Christ who will conquer both of these Emperors and such like rulers in the world!

THE DELAY IN THE PAROUSIA

The Lord is coming. Is He coming quickly or with delay? Paul spoke of the coming of the Lord in the future appearing like "a thief" (1 Thess. 4:16; 5:2-3), that is unexpectedly. John spoke of Him coming "quickly" (22:7, 20). However, over two-thousand years have expired and the Lord has not returned to judge the world. The motif of delay was already at work in the present time of the New Testament among Christians and established Judaism in Revelation 6:10 (Wright 463). How can one reconcile the coming of the Lord with such delay?

The first explanation of the assumed delay is in the figure "like a thief" that Paul uses (1 Thessalonians 5:4). "He uses the word *kleptes* for "thief." The breaking in of a thief is used as a figure for something or someone meaning sudden, surprising, and unexpected; used of the *Parousia* of Christ in 1 Thessalonians 5:2" (Bauer 435). The Greek expression of a thief coming unexpectedly either in the day or night does not give the exact time (3:3; 16:15). The Lord never gave a specific day of His return, so where could there be a delay (Matt. 24:36)? There is no reference in this term to the time of coming, only in the manner of His return. The use of the present tense rather than the future emphasizes the certainty of the Lord's coming. Paul supports the personal coming of Christ as a sudden destruction upon the foes of Christianity in the final judgment!

John uses the word *tachu* four times in the Revelation in his admonition for Christ to "come quickly" (22:20). In fact, Christ who testified the things written in the Revelation, said, "Yes, I am coming quickly" (22:7, 20). He admonishes the church to be watchful for His coming "so that no one will take your crown" (2:16; 3:11). His use of the term means at once, at a rapid rate, without delay or as soon as possible (Gal. 1:6; 2 Thess. 2:2; 1 Tim. 5:22; Rev. 22:20). Paul expresses a similar desire in the Aramiaic word transliterated *Maranatha* for the Lord to come in judgment on the wicked (1 Cor. 16:22). The early believers had a sense of certainty, an eager longing, and "a hastening" for the Lord's coming to relieve suffering (cf. 2 Pet. 3:12). John was suffering when he expressed this desire which would have been a tremendous relief (1:9). The term releases the idea of delay. If the Lord waited another thousand years to come, it would be soon or without delay, as God accounts time (cf. 2 Pet. 3:8). Therefore, there is no delay in the *Parousia* of Christ!

A final response to man's assumed delay in the Second Coming of Christ should be understood in light of God's patience in sending Christ to judge the world (2:21; Rom. 2:4; cf. 2 Pet. 3:9, 15). Paul uses the word *makrothumia* meaning the longsuffering, forbearance, patience of God and Christ toward others (Rom. 9:22; 1 Tim. 1:16; 1 Pet. 3:20; 2 Pet. 3:15). God is tolerant and patient to render punishment to the wicked because of His desire for them to repent. He waited in the days of Noah while the ark was being prepared before He destroyed the world. The fact that He has not returned gives man opportunity to repent and serve Him on earth. One must heed the admonition! The judgment has been given to the Son of God, but with no word on when it will begin (John 5:22-24, 30). The time of His coming is not the most important thing at hand; it is the preparation of mankind!

THE COMING OF CHRIST IN REVELATION

The book of Revelation opens and closes with Christ promising to return to rescue the suffering saints (1:7; 22:20). This is an anchor and a stay for the believer, but it sounds an alarm and a warning for the sinner. This is Christ's last promise to the disciples. John also eagerly awaits the Second Coming of Christ. This is the last prayer of the Bible. "Come, Lord Jesus and lift the burden of the day! Come, Lord Jesus and bring an end to all sin, sorrow, suffering, sickness, and the miserable mess with which people are involved! Come, Lord Jesus and take us unto Yourself and let us abide there eternally!" Have you ever had a day in which you could and did pray this prayer?

Jesus Christ is coming again in **Person** (1 Thess. 4:16, 17). The primary meaning of *Parousia* of Christ is 'presence'. He gave the disciples hope of His return many times (Acts 1:11; John 14:1-6). He wanted them to be with Him spiritually in the Father's dwelling place.

So, He is coming to receive them at the last day. In the meantime we know how to go to Him (John 14:5-6). He will not send someone else; He will appear personally. One can be warned that there will be a judgment sentence passed on this day (John 5:22, 30). At this day every single individual will appear before Christ. However, it will be a glorious day for the redeemed (22:1-15)!

The Lord will appear **visibly** (1 Thess. 4:16). John reminds one that "every eye shall see him" (1:7). The Second Coming of Christ involves a "revelation" (2 Thess. 1:7). He will be made manifest, which means to show or reveal oneself, to appear as the Redeemer. He will be known to every person as Lord and Savior. The redeemed will meet Him in the air and will be with the Lord forever (1 Thess. 4:17, 18). Paul gave this admonition to the Thessalonians for comfort, hope, and victory. John gave this message to the seven churches of Asia for victory over persecution.

The Second Advent of Christ will be **audible** (1 Thess. 4:16). The archangel will announce His coming with a voice loud, clear, and forceful as the "trumpet of God." The living and the dead will hear the shout of the Lord's voice (John 5:28, 29). It will be sudden destruction for the wicked (1 Thess. 5:3; 2 Thess. 1:7-9). It will be victory and redemption for the saved (1 Thess. 5:9-11). Therefore, one must not sleep, but be watchful and of a sound mind to be prepared!

One can rest assured that Christ is coming again! Man is living between two advents of the Lord Jesus Christ. The First Coming is a matter of history as it continues to unfold. The Second Coming is a matter of prophecy as it points to the future. The spiritual minded person longs for, rejoices at the thought of the coming of Christ as a day of victory. Christianity is not a life of defeat, but victory and hope! The presence of Christ will glorify the suffering and tired saints, and believers will be amazed because the testimony of God was believed and obeyed (2 Thess. 1:10). Man can be in the winner's circle!

The admonition is to be patient until the coming of the Lord (2 Thess. 1:4, 10-12). The heart of every believer must be established on the teaching of Christ. The purpose of the heart must be strengthened, stable, firm, sure, and unwavering when faced with trials and persecution. Satan cannot defeat the believer! John in the Revelation is inviting Jesus to return quickly. He has suffered enough in this life (1:7, 9). He is ready to meet God and enjoy eternal victory. In this respect death is a comfort, joy, peace, and gives complete victory over sin, the world, and Satan through Jesus Christ. God is great! Life is good! Victory is possible!

HOME AT LAST!

It is a true principle of American freedom that "a man's home is his castle." Many times our freedom and security is threatened in life. However, Christ will return to destroy this world and take us home to the "new heaven and new earth" (21:1). It is comforting to know that Christ is building a home for believers that cannot be destroyed by fire, hail, or flooding, nor can it be taken by governmental force (John 14:1-6). Who knows? It may be finished now. Behold He is standing at the door and knocking for your response in order to welcome you into the eternal home at last!

"Ever since I was a boy, my dreams of travel and adventure have been balanced with a powerful sense of home, the vision of a warm center for all my roaming, the notion of a glowing hearth where I could retire after a hard day's journey to rest, to be renewed, to remind myself of who I am and what I love" (Thomas Kinkade). Jesus reminds us in the Book of Revelation that we are children of God on a journey to heaven. It is the final resting place of believers where there is no night, mourning, nor tears! God will remove all of these with His big Fatherly hand! Do you want to go?

Conclusion

The book of Revelation has much to teach one about the victory of the redeemed church through Jesus Christ. It has a message that assures the Christian of victory over the world. He can win because Christ has already conquered the world. The apocalyptic nature of this book gives it great meaning. It differs from the usual pessimistic apocalyptic literature of the world in that it is optimistic about the Messiah who had already appeared to give the ultimate victory.

The author of Revelation uses apocalyptic imagery to reveal past, present, and future events. Christ is the messianic king who fulfilled God's Old Testament promises, who comforts saints in the present, and who gives hope for the future in eschatological terms in this book. Scholars interpret the central message in the book to be the sacrificial redemptive death of Christ who overcame his enemies to give infinite comfort, hope, and victory to suffering saints. The Christology of this book is very strong. Christ was the greatest need of the early Christians.

Christ, the Lamb of God, is linked together with the Father and the Holy Spirit in the book of Revelation. This provides overwhelming evidence that the early church honored Christ in every way as fully God and man and believed him to be coreigning with God on earth and in heaven. Christ is the very source of true victory on earth and in heaven. It is physical and spiritual defeat to talk about victory without

Christ. It is recorded in the Gospel of John that Jesus told his disciples of their helplessness without him (15:18). The Christian's success disintegrates into failure if he excludes Christ and focuses attention on himself and his accomplishments. Christ is alive and in control of the lives and destiny of the saints who cry for help in persecution (6:910). Christ is the opposing power of Satan in every vision of the Revelation to comfort and reward the saints with victory.

The focus of victory in the Revelation is based on faithfulness to Christ, not the earthly circumstances in which one finds himself (22:7, 9, 12-13). Jesus Christ takes away the sins of the world and the opposition to Christianity. Victory is not always attained by those who have the greatest fortune and live in the most ideal circumstances. Victory in Christ is promised "to him who overcomes" (2:7). It is given to the faithful in the end (2:10). The words "faithful unto death" dominate the movement of the entire book. The Christian's defeats by the forces of evil are temporary. In the end the hopes and dreams of victory become a reality in Jesus Christ.

The book of Revelation goes beyond the earthly life of Christ to his final manifestation in the church and the world. It reveals what will happen to the church during her persecution. It manifests the eternal nature of the church (Dan. 2:44). It is a form of prophecy that gives knowledge of the salvation of the Christians through the death, burial, and resurrection of Christ, the Lamb of God. It is this moment in his glorious coming for which the suffering church yearns (20:17). The church through the power of Christ can clearly see that persecution is the means of victory over Satan and the world.

The contents of the Apocalypse must be understood with God's purpose in mind. That is, the seven churches of Asia are given power through Christ to overcome her enemies (2:7, 11, 26; 3:5, 12, 21). The Holy Spirit speaks a message to all the churches controlled and supported by the Son of God (1:13, 16, 20). The loyalty of the church and the universal priesthood of all believers in Christ are the assurance of final victory of faithful Christians in heaven (1:6).

In the seven letters to the churches of Asia, one can find the problems common to all of God's people and his assessment of them, with recommendations and promises of victory. The glorified Christ stands with all authority in the midst of the churches to rule and comfort the saints in persecution. He sees their condition and brings his commendations, complaints, warnings, and promises of victory to the faithful. The church grew in a dynamic way, overcoming the Roman Empire because Christ was her Lord and Jehovah was her great overseer and provider. The Holy Spirit dwelled in her during the days of persecution to provide comfort and hope of future life in heaven through the message of the Revelation.

The message of the Revelation of Jesus Christ challenges the saints to distinguish God's cause from Satan's cause in their daily lives by following Christ (17:14). Those who are called, chosen, and faithful to Christ have the victory over Satan, the source of persecution and evil in the world. They are more than conquerors in Christ, which is a theme in the New Testament and completed in the Revelation (2:10; 4:4; Rom. 8:31-39; 1 Cor. 15:57). There is hope for all believers in Christ.

Revelation is a book of hope and comfort to the saints. It is a summation of cosmic disorders that press on the church (6:12; Joel 2; Matt. 26:29f). It reveals hope for the saints in the new heavens and earth (Isa. 66; Rev. 21). It affirms that God will punish the wicked, overthrow the nations, and give the church the ultimate victory (5:11f; 16:1f; 20:7f). God is present and protects the church from the Roman Empire. The church celebrates with Christ, the King of kings, in heaven over the fall of Rome (19:1-21). The rights of the saints were "avenged" or vindicated by Christ (19:2; 6:10). They praise God throughout eternity for deliverance from persecution. Christ and his followers are given a celebration supper because all enemies were defeated.

The Apocalypse is a unique book filled with mystery. The message was conveyed by visions and symbols. The vision of God on his heavenly throne is a beautiful picture of the victory and worship of the saints (4:15, 14). The visions and symbols are also understood in the use of the number seven, such as seven churches (1:4), seven seals (6:18:5), seven trumpets of judgment (8:6-11:18), seven thunders

(10:3f), seven major personages (12:17), seven books of wrath (15:1-16:21), and the seven beatitudes (1:3; 14:13); 16:15; 19:9; 20:6; 22:7, 14). The symbolism of the series of sevens pictures the complete judgment of God on the enemies of the church.

The book closes with the final testimony of Christ to the saints (22:6-21). The saved finally have eternal security and fellowship with God (22:5). Christ gave John a book that is faithful and true (22:69). The words of Christ to the saints are reliable and trustworthy. The actual facts of this book are true and genuine for the present situation of the saints. Victory in heaven is the blessing for those who faithfully keep the words of this prophecy.

Christ gave three warnings and promises to the saints in his conclusion (22:10-15). First, he warned them of his second coming (22:10-12). Second, he promised a reward to the faithful worker (22:12). Third, he promised entrance into the eternal city (22:14). Persecution must not stop them from preparation for heaven, but warn them of its necessity. Christ encourages the saints to work until the very end. He assures them that their labor is not in vain.

The final warning of Christ to the churches of Asia was for them to accept the message of this book (22:16-21). Christ, the Holy Spirit, and the bride, the church, invite everyone to hear, thirst for, and accept the teaching of this book of victory without addition or subtraction. Christ is the victor in the church over all enemies. The grace of Christ is with the saints on earth and in heaven.

The final admonition is that my name is in God's Book of Life (3:5; 13:8; 17:8; 20:12, 15; 21:27; 22:19). It is a blessing to live eternally in heaven where neither sin nor spiritual impurity dwells. John wrote: "Nothing impure will ever enter it, nor will anyone who does what is shameful or deceitful, but only those whose names are written in the Lamb's book of life" (21:27). "My name is in the book of Life, O bless the name of Jesus! I rise above all doubt and strife, and read my title clear" (D.S. Warren). Are you living above all doubt and fear? Can you read your title clear in heaven?

Why are people in America so distraught and distressed? America wake up! You are not led by the God of heaven. You are not following the Conqueror who is riding the white horse of victory to the throne room. Therefore, you are troubled. Christ is the worthy leader. He is leading Believers to the throne room, having conquered the power of Satan and his domain, the world. God has the last word, Come, Lord Jesus" (22:20). Praise God, we won!

Works Cited

Barabas, Steven and Tenney, Merril C. *The Zondervan Pictorial Encylopedia of the Bible, Vols. 4 and 5*. Grand Rapids: Zondervan Publishing House, 1976.

Bauer, Walter. *A Greek-Engllish Lexicon Of The New Testament*. Chicago: The University Of Chicago Press, 1957.

Berdyaev, Nicholas. *The Destiny of Man*. London: Harper Torch Publishing, 1960. Boettner, Loraine. *Immortality*. Philadelphia: The Presbyterian And Reformed Publishing Company, 1956.

_____. *Studies in Theology*. United States Of America: The Presbyterian And Reformed Publishing Company, 1974.

Brown, Colin, ed. *The New International Dictionary of New Testament Theology*. Vol. 3. Grand Rapids: Zondervan Publishing House, 1978.

Bown, Jennifer. *Interpretation A Journal Of Bible And Theology*. 54, No. 4. Richmond, Virginia: Union Theological Seminary, October 2000.

Bullock, Hassell C. *An Introduction to the Old Testament Poetic Books*. Chicago: Moody Press, 1979.

Coffman, Burton James. *Commentary on Leviticus and Numbers*. Abilene, Texas: A. C. U. Press, 1987.

Day, George E. *Theology Of The Old Testament*. Grand Rapids:

Zondervan Publishing House, ND.

Douglas, J. D. and Tenney, Merrill C. *The New International Dictionary Of The Bible*. Grand Rapids: Zondervan Publishing House, 1987.

Echols, Eldred. *Haven't You Heard? There's a War Going On!*. Fort Worth, Texas: Sweet Publishing, 1992.

Elwell, Walter A. *Baker Theological Dictionary Of The Bible*. Grand Rapids: Baker Books, 1996.

Fee, Gordon D and Stuart, Douglas. *How To Read The Bible For All Its Worth: A Guide To Understanding The Bible*. Grand Rapids: Zondervang Publishing House, 1993.

Ferguson, Everett. *The Revelation To John (The Apocalypse*. Abilene, TX: Abilene Christian University Press, 1974.

Francis, James Allen. "One Solitary Life", Essay in *The Real Jesus and Other Sermons*. Philadelphia: Judson Press, 1926.

Gese, Hartmut. *Essays On Biblical Theology*. Minneapolis: Augsburg Publishing House, 1981.

Gibbon, Edward. *The Decline And Fall Of The Roman Empire*. New York: Harcourt, Brace, and Company, 1960.

Green, Thomas Shelton. *A Greek-English Lexicon To The New Testament*. Grand Rapids: Zondervan Publishing House, 1970.

Guthrie, Donald. *The Relevance Of John's Apocalypse*. Grand Rapids: William B. Eerdmans Publishing Company, 1987.

Guinness, Alma E. *Mysteries of the Bible*. New York: The Reader's Digest Association, Inc., 1988.

Hagglund, Bengt. Translated by Gene J. Lund. *History Of Theology*. Saint Louis: Concordia Publishing House, 1966.

Hendrikson, William. *More Than Conquerors an Interpretation of the Book of Revelation*. Grand Rapids: Baker Book House, 1967.

Hesse, Brian and Wapnish, Paul. *Near Eastern Archaeology*. 63, No. 4.
    Birmingham: Alabama: University of Alabama, December 2000.

Hodge, Charles. *Systematic Theology Volume Three*. Grand Rapids:
    William B. Eerdmans Publishing Company, 1975.

House, Paul R. *Old Testament Theology*. Downers Grove, Illinois:
    InterVarsity Press, 1998.

Humes, James C. *The Wit and Wisdom of Winston Churchill*. New York:
    Harper Perennial, 1994.

Irenaeus, *Adversus Haereses* 5.29.2 and 5.30.3. Translated by A.
    Cleveland Cox. Vol. 1, *The Ante-Nicene Fathers*. Grand Rapids:
    William B. Eerdmans Publishing Company, 1985.

Kerr, Hugh T. *Reading In Christian Thought*. Nashville: Abingdon Press,
    1990. Kiefer, Otto. *Sexual Life In Ancient Rome*. New York:
    Barnes and Noble, Inc., 1962.

Kittel, Gerhard. *Theological Dictionary of the New Testament*. Grand
    Rapids: William Eerdmans Publishing Company, 1967.

Knight, Phil. *A Letter to The Author*. Beaver, OR: Nike, Inc. December
    5, 1995.

Kostenberger, Andrews J. *Journal of the Evangelical Theological
    Society, Vol. 47, No. 4*. Wake Forest, North Carolina: Southern
    Baptist Theological Seminary, December 2004.

Leivstad, Ragnar. *Christ The Conqueror, Ideas of Conflict and Victory in
    the New Testament*. New York: The MacMillian Company, 1954.

Lockyer, Herbert. *All The Doctrines Of The Bible*. Grand Rapids:
    Zondervan Publishing House, 1976.

Martin, J. L. *The Voice of the Seven Thunders or Lectures On The
    Apocalypse*. Bedford, Ind.: James M. Mathes Publishers, 1873.

Mattox, F. W. *The Eternal Kingdom*. Delight, Arkansas: Gospel Light
    Publishing Company, 1961.

M'Clintock, John and Strong, James. *Cyclopedia Of Biblical, Theological, And Ecclesiastical Literature, Vol 1, 2, 7, 8.* Grand Rapids: Baker Book House, 1973.

Morris, Leon. *The Epistle To The Romans.* Grand Rapids: William B. Eerdmans Publishing Company, 1988.

_____. *1 and 2 Thessalonians.* Grand Rapids: William B. Eerdmans Publishing company, 1984.

_____. *Revelation.* Grand Rapids: William B. Eerdmans Publishing Company, 1990. Myers, Allen C. *The Eerdmans Bible Dictionary.* Grand Rapids: William B. Eerdmans Publishing company, 1987.

Osborne, Grant R. *The Hermeneutical Spiral A Comprehensive Introduction to Biblical Interpretation.* Downers Grove, Illinois: InterVarsity Press, 1991.

Patton, John H. " John F. Kennedy Inaugural Address" in *Quarterly Journal of Speech*, Vol. 65, Issue 3. Oxford, UK: Routledge, 1979.

Penna, Romano. Translated by Thomas P. Wahl. *Paul The Apostle Jew and Greek Alike A Theological Study.* Collegeville, Minnesata: The Liturgical Press, 1996.

Perez, William D. http://www.nikebiz,com. "Overview/History/195s. html, Accessed May 2, 2011.

Philo. *On Dreams.* 1:256. Pfeiffer, Charles F. *Baker's Bible Atlas.* Grand Rapids: Baker book House, 1973.

Plevnik, Joseph. *Paul and the Parousia An Exegetical And Theological Investigation.* Peabody, Massachusetts: Hendrickson Publishers, 1997.

Ramsey, W. M. *The Letters To The Seven Churches Of Asia.* New York: A. C. Armstrong and Son, 1905.

Ridderbos, Herman. Translated by John Richard DE Witt. *Paul An*

Outlilne of His Theology. Grand Rapids: William B. Eerdmans Publishing Company, 1975.

Rissi, Mathias. "The Rider on the White Horse" in *Interpretation: A Journal of Bible And Theology.* (October 1964).

Robertson, A. T. *Word Pictures in the New Testament, Vol. IV The Epistles Of Paul.* Nashville: Broadman Press, 1931.

Schlatter, Adolf. *The Theology of the Apostles The Development of New Testament Theology.* Grand Rapids: Baker Books, 1998.

Schmidt, F. Wessel. *Concordia Journal.* Saint Louis: Concordia Seminary, October 2001.

Scott, H. G. Liddell and R. *A Greek-English Lexicon.* Oxford: Clarendon, 1966.

Stott, John R. W. *The Letters Of John.* Grand Rapids: William B. Eerdmans Publishing Company, 1996.

Strauss, James D. *The Seer, the Saviour, and The Saved; The Lord of the Future.* Joplin, Missouri: College Press, 1972.

Summers, Ray. *Worthy is the Lamb.* Nashville, Tennessee: Broadman Press, 1951.

Swete, H.B. *Commentary On Revelation.* Grand Rapids: Kregel Publications, 1977.

Talbert, Charles H. *Reading John.* New York: Crossroad Publishing Company, 1994.

Tennant, Agnieszka. *Christianity Today. Vol. 48, No. 10.* Carol Stream: Illinois: Paul D. Robbinson, October 2004.

Thayer, Joseph Henry. *A Greek-English Lexicon of the New Testament.* Grand Rapids: Zondervan Publishing House, 1975.

Tenney, Merrill C., ed. The Zondervan Pictorial Encyclopedia of the Bible, vol. 2 and 3. Grand Rapids: Zondervan Publishing House, 1976.

Vine, W. E. *Vine's Complete Expository Dictionary Of Old And New Testament Words*. New York: Thomas Nelson Publishers, 1985.

Wolpe, David J. *Why Faith Matters*. New York: HarperCollins, 2008.

Wright, N. T. *The New Testament And The People Of God, Vol. One*. Minneapolis: Fortress Press, 1992.

Young, Edward J. *The Prophecy of Daniel: A Commentary*. Grad Rapids: William B. Eerdmans Publishing Company, 1949.

Young, Robert. *Analytical Concordance to the Bible*. Grand Rapids: William B. Publishing Company, 1971.

About The Author

Roger E. Shepherd with his wife and devoted companion, Sharon Mitchell Shepherd for 37 years, live in Montgomery, AL. They have two children, Jason Shepherd and Lori Shepherd Harp. They have two precious grandchildren, Jacob and Jesse Harp.

Roger received his formal education Heritage Christian University (Bachelor of Arts, 1988), David Lipscomb University (Master of Arts, 1995), and Fuller Theological Seminary (Doctor of Missiology, 2010). He serves as Dean of the College of General Studies and professor at Amridge Univeristy, Montgomery. AL.

Dr. Shepherd has been involved in mission work in several states in the United States, as well as Germany, New Zealand, Barbados, the Ukraine, and Tanzania. He served for one year as Vice-President and Director of Evangelism and Missions at World Bible Institute, in McDonough, GA. He presently serves as Dean of the College of General Studies and professor of missions at Amridge University, Montgomery, AL.

Dr. Shepherd is the author of a manual on personal evangelism entitled *Personal Evangelism: One Winning One*. He also edited *Missions: Rekindling the Fire* with Dr. J. J. Turner, and plans to further teach and write in the field of missiology as God leads. ProQuest has just published his dissertation entitled *Leadership Patterns in Growing Churches of* Christ. He has twelve years teaching experience and forty years preaching, ministry, and mission experience. He specializes in the areas of personal evangelism, missions, and leadership both in the local church and foreign mission fields. He participates in mission trips each year which brings a rich field experience to the students. He also conducts workshops, lectures, and writings for the local church. He is also a capable teacher in the biblical text of the Old and New Testaments.